KINGS, LOVERS
& FOOLS

KINGS, LOVERS & FOOLS

JOHANNA JOHNSTON

SCHOLASTIC BOOK SERVICES
New York Toronto London Auckland Sydney Tokyo

ISBN 0-590-30954-4 (Student Edition)
ISBN 0-590-31821-7 (Teacher Edition)

Copyright © 1980 by Johanna Johnston. All rights reserved. Published by Scholastic Book Services, a Division of Scholastic Magazines, Inc.

12 11 10 9 8 7 6 5 4 3 2 1   9   0 1 2 3 4 5/8

CONTENTS

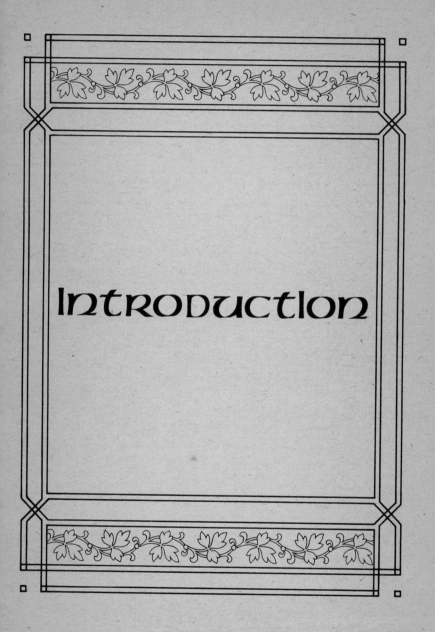

INTRODUCTION

IT IS AMAZING how little we know about the man considered the greatest English dramatist of all time. He was born in 1564—a few years after Elizabeth I had become queen—in the little town of Stratford-on-Avon, not many miles from London. He probably went to the local grammar school but surely he could not have learned there the fabulous vocabulary, the history, the literary allusions that fill his plays and poetry.

At the age of 18, he married a local girl, Anne Hathaway. They had children, a daughter named Susanna, twins named Hamnet and Judith. What he did for the next few years to support his family, no one knows.

Then sometime in his middle twenties he went to London and found the theater, which became his world. There are legends about how he started as a call boy or by holding gentlemen's horses outside the theater but there is no proof for any of these tales. All we really know is that by 1592, when Shakespeare was twenty-eight, he was not only acting with a London company, he had also begun to write dramas of his own for the company to perform.

Scholars have spent years of research and effort trying to fix the exact dates of all the plays Shakespeare wrote, a difficult task, for Shakespeare was not writing them for publication. He was simply writing them, as fast as he could, so that the acting company of which he was a member would have new and exciting plays with which to lure customers. For inspiration, he read histories, romances, plays by European writers. Anything that came his way he devoured, reworked, or used as a starting point.

And so it came about that in the next twenty years he wrote more than thirty dramas which won him a reputation not only with playgoers but with his writing colleagues as well. He also made enough money so that he could buy various properties back home in Stratford-on-Avon. Then, at the early age of 49, he left the theatrical world which had fused him with such creative excitement and retired to Stratford-on-Avon to live as a gentleman farmer. He died there in 1616 at the age of 52.

Well, there are more facts to discover, of course. One can read about the London of Shakespeare's time, learn about the streets he walked. One can read about the London acting companies, and learn how men and boys played all the female parts in those days, and how a flag went up over the theater to signify an afternoon's performance. One can learn lots of interesting things.

Still, the man himself remains a mystery, revealed only in the beauty of the poetry he wrote, the amazing insights into human character that his dramas show, and the sweep of action and excitement he brought to all his work.

If it seems presumptuous to try to condense the genius of Shakespeare, the only excuse is that these brief synopses of a few of his plays may encourage some readers to find Shakespeare's riches for themselves in their entirety.

macbeth

hE HAD NEVER thought of being a king. He was Macbeth, thane, or lord, of Glamis, general in the army, a bluff, fighting man who served his country by beating back the Norsemen who tried, every so often, to invade Scotland. And that was enough for him.

And then the witches spoke.

He and Banquo, another general, were on their way home after another successful skirmish with the Norsemen. And Macbeth was especially pleased with the whole affair because he had finally exposed the treasonous activities of the thane of Cawdor and seen him taken prisoner.

They were crossing a plain when they saw the witches—three weird sisters—chanting and dancing in a circle.

Macbeth and Banquo stopped, amazed. Who were these creatures? Were they real? "Speak if you can," said Macbeth. "What are you?"

The witches spoke—in turn.

"Hail, Macbeth, thane of Glamis!"

"All hail Macbeth, thane of Cawdor!"

"All hail Macbeth who shall be king hereafter."

Macbeth was too bewildered to speak, but Banquo had something to say. These were fine predictions for Macbeth. Did the witches have any prophecies for him?

"Hail," they said.

"Lesser than Macbeth and greater."

"Thou shalt get kings, though thou be none."

With that, the witches vanished, leaving Macbeth and Banquo to stare at each other, repeating some of their words. "Your children shall be kings," said Macbeth. Banquo answered, "You shall *be* king. And thane of Cawdor too…"

But surely this was some sort of evil magic, not to be trusted. They shook their heads and started on their way again.

They had not gone far when two of their lieutenants came hurrying after them, excited by their news. The king had stripped the traitorous thane of Cawdor of his title and his lands and named Macbeth thane of Cawdor in his stead.

It was enough to stagger anybody, coming so quickly after the prediction of the witches. Only moments before, the witches had hailed Macbeth as thane of Cawdor. So next, next...if the witches were to be believed. No, Macbeth refused to think about it. "If chance will have me king, why chance may crown me, without my stir," he muttered.

But the seed had been sown in Macbeth's mind. He was to be king someday—king as well as thane of Glamis and Cawdor.

King Duncan gave a great banquet at his palace at Dunsinane to celebrate the latest victory. He was lavish in his praise of Macbeth. But before the evening was over he named his oldest son, Malcolm, to be Prince of Cumberland. Macbeth—watching, listening—thought, there was someone else between him and the crown. Then he was horrified by his own black and deep desires.

That night he wrote to his wife, Lady Macbeth, telling her of the witches' predictions and how much had already come true.

Lady Macbeth paced up and down the hall of Inverness castle, reading and re-reading the letter. Her mind was aflame. The spirits had said that her husband would be king. Yes, she thought, yes! And she wondered how that goal might be achieved quickly. She knew her husband was an ambitious man, fearless on the battlefield, but sometimes inclined to hesitate in other areas, brooding on right and wrong. She would stiffen his courage, she thought. She was someone who could stifle remorse. She was no gentle woman—no. She was stronger than most women, stronger than Macbeth. "Come, thick night," she cried, "that my keen knife see not the wound it makes…"

Suddenly, Macbeth was home at Inverness and hurrying across the hall to her.

"Ah, great Glamis, worthy Cawdor," she said, "and greater than both thereafter. Your letters have transported me."

"My dearest love," said Macbeth, embracing her. "King Duncan will be here tonight."

"Ah," she said, "and leave when?"

"Tomorrow morning, he proposes."

Lady Macbeth shook her head slowly. "No, Duncan shall not see that morrow."

Then she saw the look of shock on Macbeth's face. "Ah, my thane, your face gives everything away. I will say no more now. Be a good host to the king. We will talk later. Meantime, leave everything to me."

And so when the king arrived—along with his sons, Malcolm and Donalbain, General Banquo, and other officers—Lady Macbeth and her husband greeted them graciously. Soon all were feasting at a lavish banquet.

But before long Macbeth stole away from the festivities to ponder alone in an empty room. His wife's plan had a horrid fascination for him. "If it were done…then 'twere well it were done quickly," he muttered. Then he shuddered. "No, no." King Duncan was a guest in his home. He had always been kind to Macbeth. More than that, he was a good king. There was no reason to wish him dead—none at all—except Macbeth's own ambition to take his place.

Lady Macbeth came in from the banquet hall. "Why are you out here?" she asked.

"We will proceed no further in this business," said Macbeth abruptly.

Lady Macbeth stared at him. It was as she had feared. In any action that did not have to do with war he was going to back away. She began to shame him. "Are you a man?" she asked. "You say you would—and then say you can't." She went on and on and her voice almost hypnotized her husband.

Finally, he said faintly, "But if we should fail?"

"But screw your courage to the sticking place and we'll not fail!" said Lady Macbeth. Then, in a low voice, she told him how the murder would be done. King Duncan would be deeply asleep after his tiring day. His two watchmen would be drugged. It would be simple then to kill the king, smear some of his blood on the watchmen, and leave their daggers by them to prove their guilt.

At last Macbeth was nodding agreement. His wife was stronger than he. He could not resist her.

Late that night, Banquo was walking in the castle courtyard, a servant beside him, carrying a torch. He felt uneasy; he did not know why. He heard footsteps and turned and saw Macbeth.

"What? Are you too awake? The king is long asleep." Then, more softly, he said, "I dreamed last night of the three weird sisters."

Macbeth said shortly, "I think not of them."

"But to you they have showed some truth," said Banquo.

Macbeth did not want to talk about that just now. Perhaps some other time.

Soon Banquo was saying good night and going into the castle to bed.

Macbeth was left alone in the courtyard, alone with the horror of what he planned to do in the next hour. He shivered and it seemed that something glimmered before his eyes.

"Is this a dagger that I see before me, the handle toward my hand? Come, let me clutch thee…" He tried to shake away the fancy and then he seemed to see the dagger dripping with blood. "Oh, oh," he moaned, "it is this bloody business ahead of me that fills me with these visions."

He heard a bell strike within the castle. It was the signal he and Lady Macbeth had agreed upon. "I go," he said, "and it is done."

How much later was it? Half an hour—an hour? Macbeth came staggering back into the courtyard where Lady Macbeth was waiting for him.

"I have done the deed," he panted, and he looked at his bloody hands, holding two daggers.

But why had he not left the daggers by the sleeping watchmen, asked Lady Macbeth. "Go, smear the sleeping grooms with blood," she said.

"I'll go no more," said Macbeth. "I am afraid to think what I have done. Look on't again I dare not."

"Oh, infirm of purpose," cried Lady Macbeth, taking the daggers from him. If he would not, then she would. Off she went, leaving Macbeth to tremble and start at every sound. He heard a knocking at the outer doors. Who could that be at this time of night? He looked about and realized that the night was almost over. A gray light showed the coming of dawn.

Lady Macbeth came hurrying from one of the castle doors. She held up her hands, bloody as Macbeth's. "My hands are your color now but I shame to wear a heart so white."

The knocking at the outer doors was repeated. Who could it be?

"Come," said Lady Macbeth. "We must wash our hands and get on our night gowns so as to be as surprised as any, whatever happens."

MACBETH

Macbeth followed his wife to the inner door leading to their
rooms. He heard the knocking again. "Ah," he said, "wake
Duncan with your knocking. I would you could."

Finally, a sleepy porter went to answer the knocking at the
great door. Two noblemen, Macduff and Lennox, were there,
cheerful in the early-morning air. Why was everyone still
asleep? they asked. Had there been a big party the night
before?

The porter went to summon Macbeth and he came out as if
just awakened from sleep and greeted the two noblemen. Macduff explained that the king had asked him to an early meeting
so Macbeth walked with him to the door of the king's chambers
and then came back to speak with Lennox.

They had only said a few words to each other when Macduff
came running out of the king's chambers crying, "Horror, horror, horror!"

"What is it? What has happened?" Macbeth tried to sound
as surprised and alarmed as Lennox.

"The king! Murdered!" Macduff cried. "Murdered. Murdered!"

"No!" cried Macbeth and Lennox together, and they ran to
the king's rooms to see for themselves.

Left alone in the anteroom, Macduff shouted for the servants. "Ring the alarum bell. Murder and treason! Banquo and
Donalbain! Malcolm! Awake!"

Soon the great bell was setting up a clamor and footsteps
were running toward the anteroom.

Lady Macbeth hurried in, asking what was wrong.

Banquo, Malcolm, and Donalbain rushed in.

"Murder!" said Macduff. "The king has been murdered!"

"Oh, no! Oh, woe!" Everyone was lamenting and asking
questions. "When?" "How?" "Who did it?"

Just then, Macbeth ran in, his hands bloody.

"Oh, I do repent me, but I have killed them both. But rage overcame me when I saw those set to guard him smeared with blood—his blood...."

Lady Macbeth made as if to faint and was helped away by a servant. The others stared at each other, horrified by the bloody events of the night and morning. What was to be done now? Banquo said they must all meet later to consider.

But as Macbeth, Macduff, Lennox, and Banquo hurried away, the king's sons, Malcolm and Donalbain, remained behind. Terrible suspicions filled their minds. More was at work here than met the eye, more than they could discuss here. Perhaps, they whispered, it would be wise for them to leave the country for a while. One of them to Ireland, one to England. They did not bother to say good-bye to Macbeth, but just gathered their belongings and serving men and were soon on their way.

The ease with which Macbeth was now accepted and crowned King of Scotland was almost magical. Within days after the death of Duncan, he and Lady Macbeth were moving into the palace at Dunsinane, new king and queen of the realm. As was fitting on such an occasion, a great feast was prepared and invitations sent out to everyone of importance.

He—Macbeth—was king, just as the witches had prophesied. But he felt none of the elation he had thought he would. Instead his days and nights were full of anxious suspicions. And now most of his suspicions centered on Banquo. Banquo had been with him when the witches first spoke, and Banquo was showing in various ways *his* suspicions that Macbeth had helped at least one prophecy come true. This could not go on. Macbeth shuddered as he realized there was really only one way to end Banquo's threat. And only one way to deal with that other prediction of the witches, that Banquo's sons should be kings.

Macbeth was quicker to act than he had been previously. He found two ruffians and hired them to kill Banquo and his son, Fleance, as they came through the palace courtyard on their way to the banquet.

But then, as always, he had to brood a little. He thought of the dead King Duncan and wondered if he now had the best of it. "After life's fitful fever he sleeps well."

But the die was cast. It was time to join Lady Macbeth and welcome the guests to the feast. The banquet hall was blazing with torch light, crowded with thanes and their ladies, bowing and murmuring as King Macbeth entered and greeted them.

Just then Macbeth saw one of his hired killers at a side door. He hurried to him. Was the deed done? Well, yes and no. Banquo had been killed but his son had escaped.

"Come to the feast, my lord," called Lady Macbeth. "Our guests are waiting."

As if in a dream, Macbeth moved toward his seat at the high table. Suddenly he started in terror. Someone was sitting in his seat. It was Banquo; no, the ghost of Banquo!

"No, no," cried Macbeth. "Do not shake your gory locks at me."

Everyone looked where Macbeth was looking but no one saw the ghost except Macbeth. "Look!" Macbeth cried. "Look! There he is."

Lady Macbeth hurried to explain her husband's strange behavior. This was a kind of momentary fit to which he had been subject since his youth.

Just then the ghost vanished. Macbeth sighed with relief, sat down, and urged his guests to eat and drink.

Then the ghost appeared again.

"Go! Go!" cried Macbeth, jumping to his feet. "You are dead—your blood is cold. Do not glare at me."

By this time there was real confusion at the tables as men and women looked at each other, frowning and questioning.

Lady Macbeth raised her voice. She begged her guests' pardon for ending the banquet so abruptly but she urged them all to leave so she could put her husband to bed.

After that appearance at the banquet, Banquo's ghost did not trouble Macbeth again. But by now, he had other worries. Word came to Dunsinane that King Duncan's oldest son, Malcolm, was in England and had won the favor of the English king. There was also word that Macduff and various other Scotsmen were joining him there and it seemed likely that the English king would help them if they marched against Macbeth in an attempt to overthrow him.

What should Macbeth do? What were his chances? The tormented king decided to call upon the three witches to predict for him once again.

The witches were in a cavern, stirring some mixture in a cauldron and chanting, "Double, double, toil and trouble, fire burn and cauldron bubble. . ." They broke off as they heard someone knock. "By the pricking of my thumbs, something wicked this way comes . . . Open, locks, whoever knocks."

So the door opened for Macbeth. He entered and demanded that the witches make new predictions for him.

They waved their arms and as ghostly visions appeared against the smoky depths of the cavern, they made three prophecies.

"Beware Macduff," they said. "Beware the thane of Fife."

But then they said, "None of woman born can harm Macbeth."

Finally, "Macbeth can never vanquished be until Great Birnam Wood to high Dunsinane hill shall come against him."

With that they vanished into the smoky gloom of the cave.

"Beware Macduff." The words rang in Macbeth's overheated mind. Well, Macduff was in England now, but he could swoop down on Macduff's castle and wipe out all his family so there would be none of Macduff's line to threaten him. He rushed off to give orders for the seizing of Macduff's castle and the killing of his wife and children before his terrible resolve could weaken.

A few days later, a messenger from Scotland took the news of the slaughter to Macduff in England. He and Malcolm had been discussing when it might be wise to launch their attack on Macbeth. At this awful news, they sprang to their feet. The time had come. "Macbeth is ripe for shaking," said Malcolm. "The powers above will help us. Come, the night is long that never finds the day."

Strangely, Lady Macbeth, who had been so resolute when King Duncan was to be murdered, had become distraught after her husband's latest killings. She was quiet and still during the days, but at night she walked in her sleep. Her maid, alarmed, brought a doctor to watch one night. And then it was just as the maid had said. Lady Macbeth rose from her bed and walked in a trance, holding a taper. Then she put the taper down and began rubbing her hands together as though washing them.

"Out, damned spot, out, I say!" she murmured as she scrubbed at her hands. Then, "The thane of Fife had a wife. Where is she now? What, will these hands ne'er be clean? Here's the smell of blood still."

The doctor shook his head. He had never seen such a case. There was nothing he could do. Good night, poor lady.

Macbeth's rule in Scotland had now become so ruthless that a great many Scotsmen were ready to join with the Scottish and English forces making their way north from England.

Macbeth raged around his well-fortified palace of Dunsinane. "No," he shouted, "bring me no more reports about how strong the English are . . . No man that's born of woman shall ever have power over me." And then, as the messengers still came, saying that the English mustered ten thousand, he shook his sword at them, waving them away. "I will not be afraid of death and bane till Birnam forest come to Dunsinane."

And now, as it happened, the English and Scottish forces were meeting at the edge of Birnam Wood to prepare for their attack on Dunsinane. It occurred to Malcolm that it might be a good idea to conceal their numbers as they marched on the palace. "Let every soldier hew him down a bough and bear it before him," he said.

The soldiers went to work, cutting boughs. Soon they were moving toward Dunsinane behind their camouflage.

At Dunsinane, Macbeth was brought the news that Lady Macbeth was dead. He held his head in his hands. "She should have died hereafter . . . Tomorrow and tomorrow and tomorrow, creeps in this petty pace from day to day, and all our yesterdays have lighted fools the way to dusty death . . ." And then, as a sort of farewell, he was murmuring, "Out, out, brief candle . . ."

The messenger that ran in now stood before him panting. Finally Macbeth looked up. "What is it? Speak." At last the messenger regained his breath. He had been looking toward Birnam and it seemed he saw the forest moving.

Macbeth jumped to his feet. "If you speak false—" he began.

But soon he saw it was all too true. The second of the witches' prophecies was being fulfilled. Birnam Wood was coming to Dunsinane.

Macbeth rushed to ring the alarum bell and rally his men. They ran forth from their posts in and around the castle and were ready to meet the advancing forces when they threw aside their concealing branches and drew their swords.

The battle was fierce. The advantage went now this way, now that. But Macbeth was everywhere, fearless and deadly.

Then he came upon Macduff. "Beware Macduff," the witches had said, but Macbeth faced him too without fear. Sure that he led a charmed life, he challenged him. "Only to a man not born of woman can I be victim."

Macduff cried hoarsely, "And now despair your charm. Know that Macduff was from his mother's womb untimely ripped."

Macbeth stared. Then he raised his sword, as Macduff's sword also flashed. What was to be must be. "Lay on, Macduff," he cried, "and damned be him that first cries 'Hold, enough!'"

He did not cry "Hold." He fought to the end and Macduff prevailed. He fell under Macduff's sword and Macduff avenged his wife and children as he cut off Macbeth's head.

It was a terrible end for a man who had done terrible deeds in pursuit of a crown. But there was only rejoicing as Macduff brought the head back to Malcolm and all the men around him.

"Hail, king," said Macduff to Malcolm, "for so thou art now with the usurper gone. Hail, King of Scotland."

Malcolm gave his thanks to Macduff and to all who had supported him and invited them to his crowning at Scone.

And so, most of the witches' prophecies came true. But as to whether some of Banquo's sons became kings later, this story does not say.

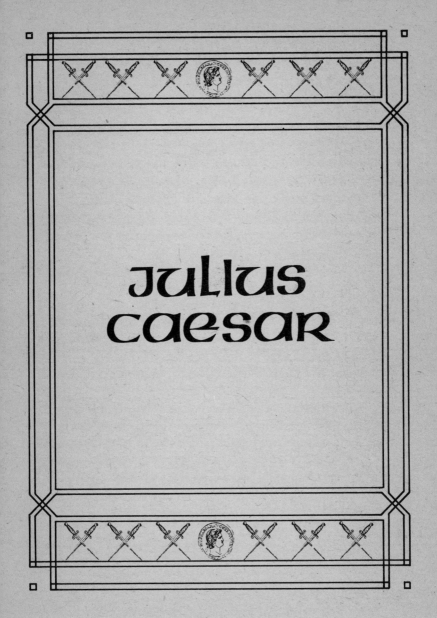

JULIUS CAESAR

T WAS A sort of holiday in Rome. Caesar, the great Julius Caesar, had returned from still another military triumph. Pale, erect, gray-haired, he walked toward the Forum surrounded by friends, and trailed by a crowd of citizens. Everyone was excited, chattering about the races that were to be run around the Palatine Hill, and speculating on what honors might be awarded Caesar after his latest successes.

Suddenly a shrill voice called over the babble. "Caesar!"

Caesar looked around. "Who calls?"

The voice shrilled again. "Beware the Ides of March!"

Caesar frowned. "What man is that? Bring him before me."

A gaunt man in a dark robe was brought before him. "He is a soothsayer, Caesar," someone said.

Caesar looked at the man. "Speak once again."

Now the soothsayer's voice was quieter as he looked into Caesar's eyes. "Beware the Ides of March."

Caesar stared at the man for a moment, then smiled. "He is a dreamer. Let us go on." He began walking again and so did the friends around him and the throng that followed.

Except for two. Brutus stepped away from Caesar's side, and in a moment, Cassius followed him.

"Not going to the races?" asked Cassius.

"Not I," said Brutus. "I am not such a gamesome fellow as Marc Antony, who likes to run."

They were silent a moment. Then Cassius asked Brutus what was troubling him. He had been very silent and depressed of late. Brutus answered slowly. He was sorry if he had seemed distant. He was really only vexed and disappointed with himself. He had accomplished so little of what he had hoped to do.

"Ah," said Cassius. It was just the opening he was waiting for. Quietly, he said that there were many noble Romans who were not very happy with the way things were going these days. They were aware of Brutus's talents which, if things were different, might be better used.

Brutus looked sharply at Cassius. What was he really saying?

Suddenly they heard shouts and trumpets in the distance.

"What does that mean?" asked Brutus. "I do fear the people choose Caesar for their king."

"Ah," said Cassius. "You fear it. And so I must think you would not have it so."

"I would not," said Brutus, "though I love Caesar well."

Cassius began to speak in a low, rapid voice. Yes, he said, yes, too many people were beginning to regard Caesar as a god. Sometimes he seemed to regard himself as one.

There was another great shout in the distance, and another flourish of trumpets.

"More honors for Caesar, I suppose," said Brutus.

Cassius nodded. "He doth bestride the narrow world like a Colossus, and we petty men walk under his huge legs and peep about . . . And why? Why he—and not you or I? The fault, dear Brutus, is not in our stars, but in ourselves, that we are underlings." Wrapped up in the subject, he asked on what meat Caesar fed that he grew so great and what was wrong with Rome that it now had room in it for only one man.

Another shout and flourish of trumpets interrupted them. And then Cassius began talking again. He did not put into words all that was in his mind but Brutus could tell what he was suggesting. There was only one way that Caesar could be toppled from the godlike position to which he had been elevated.

Then Brutus motioned Cassius to be silent. Caesar and his followers were returning from the Forum. Caesar halted a moment, looking over at Cassius and Brutus. He spoke to Marc Antony, who was beside him. "Yon Cassius has a lean and hungry look; he thinks too much. Such men are dangerous."

Antony was surprised. Cassius was a loyal Roman. How could he be dangerous?

Caesar shook his head. "Such men as he be never at heart's ease while they behold a greater than themselves, and therefore are they very dangerous." Then he turned and walked on.

Meantime, Cassius had pulled at the cloak of one of the men near Caesar, a longtime, blunt-spoken friend named Casca, and had drawn him over to the wall where Brutus stood.

"What was all the shouting about?" Cassius asked.

"Why, Antony was offering a crown to Caesar, and he refused it," said Casca. "Aye, three times he offered it and three times Caesar refused, though, indeed, it seemed he did so more slowly each time."

"And for this they cheered?"

"Some cheered that the crown was offered. Some that Caesar refused it."

"Ah!" said Cassius. He liked it that there were still Romans who resisted making Caesar a king. He asked Casca to have dinner with him the next night. They could talk further. He looked at Brutus. Brutus said that he would be at home all the next day if Cassius wanted to speak to him further. And so they all parted.

The Ides of March. It was only a division in the Roman calendar, marked by the fifteenth of March. But the night before this particular fifteenth a storm swept down like none Rome had seen before. Lightning flashed blue, green, and white; thunder crashed and rumbled. Now and then a wild wind blew, toppling trees and sending loose articles flying. But strangely enough, little rain fell.

In this frightening weather, few people were out of doors. But

Cassius, "lean and hungry Cassius," was, and so was Casca. They met on a dark street that was illuminated now and then by lightning flashes. Cassius seemed to enjoy the storm. He was excited too by other reports he had heard of strange and unlikely happenings. A lion had walked by the capitol. A man had held up his hands and flames had spurted from his fingers, but he had not been burned. Cassius had even heard that here and there graves had burst open and spectres had fluttered about.

"Now, Casca," said Cassius, "I could name a man most like this dreadful night—who thunders, lightens, roars, a man no mightier than you or me, but prodigious grown and fearful as these strange eruptions are."

"You mean Caesar," said Casca.

Cassius simply held up a hand. "Surely we Romans have the strength of our ancestors to throw off such a yoke," he said.

"They say the senators mean to establish Caesar as king tomorrow," Casca said.

"Then I know where I will wear this dagger," said Cassius." A lightning flash followed his words and Casca put out his hand to take Cassius's. He would be with Cassius every step of the way. "Good, good," said Cassius, and now it was time to meet with the other like-minded Romans who were also sworn to the conspiracy. They were waiting in the Great Colonnade.

Just then they heard footsteps.

"I know those steps," said Cassius. "It is Cinna. One of us."

And indeed, it was Cinna, glad to find friends on such a night. He had just one question for Cassius. Was it possible to win Brutus to their cause? Brutus was so well-loved by almost everyone. If he took part— Cassius interrupted him. "Be content, Cinna. I have some papers here that I would have you deliver to Brutus tonight. Throw them in the window of his study. Three parts of Brutus are with us already. These papers should bring him around altogether."

Cinna took the papers. "I will go at once," he said.

"And after that, meet us at the Great Colonnades," said Cassius. Then he and Casca listened to Cinna's footsteps retreating into the night.

"Yes," said Cassius, "Brutus is so loved that what might appear an offense in us will change to virtue and worthiness in him. Now, off to the Colonnade."

It was later that night, early morning in fact, but the strange thunder and lightning continued. Brutus, unable to sleep, was walking in the orchard behind his house. He was tormented with the decision before him. He did not hate Caesar, he loved him. What he hated was the thought of what might happen to Rome and its old Republican ways—what might happen to Caesar himself if he were made king. Brutus thought that perhaps he must think of Caesar as a serpent's egg, which, if hatched, could do much harm. Then one could justify killing the serpent in its shell.

His servant came out to him with a rolled paper which he had just found on Brutus's desk. So much sheet lightning flashed across the sky that Brutus could read the letter by its light. It was an appeal from Cassius, for Brutus to remember the valor of his ancestors and awake and strike.

Brutus was still brooding over the letter when there was a knocking at the outer gate. He sent his servant to answer it. Soon all the conspirators had joined Brutus in the dark orchard —Cassius, Casca, Cinna, Cimber, and two others, named Decius and Trebonius. There was some quick, hushed talk. Should they swear an oath to their resolution? No, said Brutus. It was enough that they were all proud Romans, bound by their own honor.

Then Cassius mentioned Marc Antony. He was very close to Caesar and a shrewd contriver as well. Perhaps when they struck they should strike Marc Antony as well.

"No!" said Brutus sharply. "Then our course would seem too bloody." Besides, he added, what harm could Antony do with Caesar dead?

Finally Cassius agreed that Antony should be spared. But there was one more question. How could they be sure that Caesar would go to the capitol on the coming day? Caesar seemed to have grown more superstitious lately. There had been that warning about the Ides of March. Now Decius spoke and said he was sure he could calm Caesar's fears, if any, and interpret any omens in an optimistic way. He would go to Caesar in the morning to fetch him.

"Nay," said Cassius, "let us all go and walk with him to the capitol."

They agreed to meet at Caesar's house at eight in the morning, then said good night to Brutus and left.

Still Brutus lingered in the dark orchard. He was committed now but he was not happy about it. Suddenly, his wife Portia came toward him. "Portia," he said, "why are you out at this hour and in this weather? You are ill."

Softly, Portia tried to get Brutus to tell her what was troubling him these days. Brutus shook his head. It was nothing, nothing. But she persisted. "Dwell I but in the suburbs of your good pleasure?" she asked. "If it be no more, I am no wife." Touched by this appeal, Brutus put his arm about her and promised her that soon he would tell her everything and then he led her back into the house.

On this strange night, now merging into dawn, still another man and wife were talking in hushed tones. Calpurnia, Caesar's wife, was begging her husband not to go to the capitol that day. There had been so many evil omens. A lion had been seen in the streets; ghosts were shrieking in the cemeteries. "Please do not go," she begged.

Caesar shook his head. "Cowards die many times before their deaths; the valiant never taste of death but once…Caesar shall go forth."

A servant came in to say that the augurs had made their sacrifices and from the results it was their opinion that Caesar should not go out this day.

Calpurnia fell on her knees. "Please, Caesar, we will send Marc Antony to say you are not well. Upon my knees, I beg this of you."

Looking down at her pleading face, Caesar finally relented. He would stay home.

Just then the conspirator Decius arrived, ready to take Caesar to the senate house in the capitol.

Caesar told Decius that he was not going. Calpurnia added, "Tell them that he is sick."

"No," said Caesar, "Caesar shall not lie. I do not go because it is my will not to go. But," he added, "I would also please Calpurnia. She had a dream tonight wherein she saw my statue, which like a fountain with a hundred spouts, did run pure blood, and many Romans came and bathed their hands therein. After this dream, she begged me on her knees to stay home today."

Decius had said he could interpret any omen in a pleasing way. Now he suggested that this was a fortunate dream. Caesar's statue spouting blood simply signified that from him great Rome should receive much reviving strength.

Caesar thought about this interpretation and Decius went on. He said he was sure that the senate was going to offer the

21

crown to Caesar today, but if they heard he was not coming, they might say, "Caesar is afraid."

Suddenly Caesar's mind was made up. He was ashamed that he had yielded to Calpurnia's fears. He was going, of course.

Right on time, the rest of the conspirators appeared at Caesar's door, ready to escort him to the capitol.

Surrounded by the men he thought were his friends, Caesar made his way up the flagged walks. And perhaps he had begun to act in a kingly manner. A man tried to hand him a scroll, asking that he read it at once because it touched him most nearly. Caesar waved him away. "What touches me shall be last served," he said. Actually, the scroll listed the names of all the conspirators and begged Caesar to beware of them, but Caesar did not look at it.

Then one of the conspirators asked Caesar if he would not change his mind about the banishment of his brother, and Caesar was more lordly and autocratic than ever. Once he had made a decision, he said, he did not change his mind. He turned to walk up the senate steps.

As if that were a signal, all the conspirators snatched their daggers from under their robes and fell upon him, stabbing him wherever they could.

"Liberty!" they shouted. "Freedom! Death to tyranny!"

The sharp blades were still flashing when Caesar looked up to see Brutus bringing his dagger down.

"Et tù, Bruté?" said Caesar. "Then fall, Caesar." And with one last gasp he was dead.

Brutus spoke to the frightened and astonished onlookers. "Fly not, stand still, ambition's debt is paid."

Then he and all the other conspirators bathed their hands in Caesar's blood. "Now we will walk in the market place," said Cassius, "holding these weapons high, and cry peace, freedom, and liberty."

Now Marc Antony appeared. He had been too far from Caesar to help him when the conspirators set upon him. But he was ready to join Caesar, he said, and bared his breast to the bloody-handed men.

"No," they said. "No." Their only goal had been to strike down Caesar and his ambition. Antony was welcome to join them in setting up a new, more democratic government.

Antony bowed his head. He went so far as to shake every bloodied hand until his own was as bloodied as the others. He had only one request to make, he said. He would like to speak at Caesar's funeral.

Brutus nodded. "You shall, Marc Antony."

Cassius frowned and shook his head. Brutus spoke to him quietly. "It will be all right. I will speak first." He turned to Antony and said he could take Caesar's body and he could indeed speak at the public funeral so long as he made sure to say nothing of blame for those who had killed him.

The conspirators hurried off and Antony was left alone with Caesar's body. He bent over it, whispering that this death would be avenged. All Caesar's wounds would open and there would be an outcry up and down Italy. Yes, the words would be, "Cry havoc, and let slip the dogs of war."

A messenger came up to him. Octavius Caesar, Caesar's son, was on his way to Rome at his father's summons. Then the messenger saw the body. "Ohh—oh," he moaned.

"Yes," said Antony. "I weep also. But now hurry back to Octavius and tell him to delay his coming. With the murder of Caesar, the city is dangerous. No, wait just a moment. First help me carry Caesar to the market place, where Brutus and I will speak over his body."

The news swept through Rome. Caesar was dead! Assassinated! A crowd gathered at the Forum and, as Antony had predicted, its mood was dangerous. Brutus moved through the muttering people. "Hear me speak," he said, and he mounted the steps.

He spoke well and sensibly. He said he had loved Caesar dearly but he loved Rome more. He spoke of Caesar's ambition to rule and how that would have made slaves of them all. Gradually he won them to thinking that what he and the other assassins had done was simply for their own good.

The crowd was practically cheering Brutus when Antony appeared, along with some men bearing Caesar's body. They were in no mood to hear any praise of Caesar. "He was a tyrant!" someone cried. Brutus raised his voice and asked that no matter what they thought they should stay and hear what Antony had to say. At last, they subsided.

Antony spoke. "Friends, Romans, countrymen, lend me your ears; I come to bury Caesar, not to praise him. The evil that men do lives after them, the good is oft interred with their bones; so let it be with Caesar. The noble Brutus has told you Caesar was ambitious." If so, Antony went on, that was a grievous fault, and surely it must be so "for Brutus is an honorable man." All the conspirators were honorable men. Antony then spoke of his own love for Caesar, but Brutus said he was ambitious and Brutus was an honorable man.

Gradually, Antony began winning the crowd to him. His listeners began remembering some of the good things about Caesar that should not be buried. They began to wonder if Brutus and the other killers really were so honorable after all.

Then Antony spoke of finding Caesar's will and how they would weep to hear it and learn his love for them.

"Read the will!" "Read it!"

Antony was reluctant to do so. He spoke instead of Caesar's

love for the very men who had killed him. By now some of his listeners were in tears and others were shouting out that Caesar's death should be avenged. Antony tried to restrain them, reminding them again that Brutus and the others were all honorable men. But the fever was mounting. Antony called out, "You have forgot the will I told you of."

"Ah, the will!" "Yes, the will!" "Read the will!"

Antony read from a parchment that to every Roman citizen Caesar had bequeathed seventy-five drachmas.

A sigh breathed through the crowd. "Most noble Caesar! We will avenge him."

There was more to the will. "He also has left you all his private arbors and orchards on this side of the Tiber to be yours and your heirs', forever as a common pleasure ground."

Now there was no holding Antony's listeners. They were going to take Caesar's body to be burned in the holy place. Then with the brands from that burning they would set fire to all the homes of the traitors who had killed him."

Antony watched the mob surge forward. "Cry havoc," he had said when first looking at Caesar's body, "and let slip the dogs of war." In his quiet speech, so moderate, blaming no one, he had unleashed those dogs.

In the tumult of the next days, Brutus, Cassius, and the other conspirators fled the city. Antony, Caesar's son Octavius, and another Roman, Lepidus, took control of the government to restore order and for a while were ruthless in their commands.

But out on the plains near Sardis where Brutus, Cassius, and the others had set up camp, a small army of men sympathetic to the conspirators was gathering.

Hearing of that gathering of troops, Antony, Octavius, and Lepidus made sure that the armed forces of Rome were ready to march. The mischief begun on the Ides of March was indeed mushrooming into civil war.

At Sardis, Brutus and Cassius discussed the situation. They had learned that Antony and his troops had moved out from Rome to Philippi. Brutus was eager to go and meet them there. Cassius thought it would be wiser to let the enemy come to them. Brutus would not listen to such advice. They had a full quota of men, eager and ready. "We are at the height," he said. "There is a tide in the affairs of men, which, taken at the flood, leads on to fortune; omitted, all the voyage of their life is bound in shallows…"

So Brutus had his way. They would march tomorrow toward Philippi.

That night Brutus was wakeful long after his servants had gone to sleep. Suddenly, the candle flame flickered. A misty form took shape beyond the candlelight. Brutus felt a chill down his spine and his hair tingled. It was the ghost of Caesar.

"Why have you come?" he whispered.

The ghost answered, "To tell thee thou shalt see me at Philippi."

"Well," said Brutus, "then I shall see thee again?"

"Ay, at Philippi," answered the ghost, and then vanished.

After a moment, Brutus roused his servants. He had heard them cry out in their sleep. Had they seen anything? No, they all said. Brutus sighed. Very well. There was nothing to do now but proceed with the plan to march toward Philippi at dawn.

Two days later, the opposing armies were halted a little distance from each other on the plains of Philippi. Their generals met in the center of the field for a parley. But there was no hope of a truce. Antony and Octavius were determined to punish the men who had killed Caesar. The generals went back to their own lines.

Soon the battle was underway. Shouts, cries, and the clang of swords on shields filled the air. For a while it seemed that Brutus and Cassius and their forces were doing well. But then—did Brutus give a signal for one wing to move too soon? Cassius thought so. But there was no time for blame. Antony's men were swarming around the wing that Cassius commanded. His men were fleeing in retreat.

Cassius stood upon a little hill and saw the enemy closing in on him. He turned to his servant. "I took you a prisoner in Parthia," he said, "and when I saved your life you swore to do whatever I bid thee. Come now, and be a free man ever after. Take this sword which ran through Caesar, and when my face is covered, run it through me." Cassius covered his eyes and his servant did as he had been told. When he saw his onetime master lying dead, he turned and ran for freedom.

Things were not going well for Brutus either. Word came to Antony that he had been captured and Antony was quick to say he must not be harmed. He wanted Brutus as a friend, not an enemy.

But Brutus had not been captured. He and some of his captains were resting briefly on a little knoll, watching sadly as their men ran from the advancing enemy.

"I saw Caesar again last night," said Brutus. "I know my hour has come." And then, as shouts of "Fly, fly," came from the retreating men, he turned to his companions. "Yes, it is time for you to fly too." But as they left he beckoned to one captain to stay behind as the others left. "You are a man of good respect, Strato. Hold then my sword, and turn away thy face while I do run upon it."

"Give me your hand first," said Strato. Then, softly, "Fare you well, my lord."

Then he held the sword as Brutus requested and Brutus ran upon it saying, "Caesar, now be still; I kill'd not thee with half so good a will."

When the news of Brutus's death came to Marc Antony he was not really surprised. This was how Brutus would have gone. And now Antony had his own words of farewell for him.

> "This was the noblest Roman of them all;
> All the conspirators save only he
> Did what they did in envy of great Caesar.
> He only, in a general honest thought made one of them.
> His life was gentle, and the elements
> So mix'd in him that Nature might stand up
> And say to all the world, 'This was a man.'"

hamlet

ODDLY ENOUGH, the young prince of Denmark, Hamlet, was not the first to see his father's ghost. Two guards walking the battlements of Elsinore castle one night saw the misty figure float before them, then disappear. On another night, a school friend of Hamlet's, Horatio, and an officer named Marcellus, saw the spectre suddenly appear, seem to beckon, seem about to speak, and then when a cock crowed, it vanished.

"It is the king—the old king," said Horatio in a hushed tone. "Why does he appear?"

"Perhaps to warn us to stay alert against Fortinbras and the Norwegians," said Marcellus.

"But we seem well enough guarded," said Horatio. "I think Hamlet should hear about this. Perhaps the ghost will speak to him."

It was odd indeed that Hamlet had not heard about the ghost. He had returned to Denmark from his studies in Wittenberg at the news of his father's death, two months before. He had grieved, as any loving son would grieve for a father he admired. He wept on his mother's shoulder. He held the hands of Claudius, his father's brother, and thought they grieved together also.

Then an astonishing thing had happened. Only weeks after his father's death, Claudius, his uncle, and his mother were married.

Nobody asked Hamlet what he thought about it, coming so soon after his father's death. No one paid any attention to him during the festivities that followed the wedding. But as the days passed, people did begin to notice that Hamlet had a silent manner and a dark look.

King Claudius was a bustling, get-ahead sort of man. He sat at the long table in the great hall, his queen beside him, his courtiers around him. He listened to some advice from his lord chancellor, an elderly fellow name Polonius. He sent off messengers to Norway with a letter to young Fortinbras's uncle which he hoped would discourage any threat of invasion. He beckoned to Polonius's son, young Laertes, who had asked for a favor. He heard that Laertes wanted to return to France for a while and had won his father's permission to go if the king consented. The king gave his consent.

Finally all the business was taken care of. The king turned to Hamlet, who was slouched in a chair nearby.

"And now, my nephew Hamlet, and my son!" he said heartily.

Hamlet looked away from the king and muttered, "A little more than kin and less than kind."

The king seemed not to hear. What he—and the queen also —wanted to talk about was Hamlet's low state of mind. "How is it that the clouds still hang on you?" said Claudius, and the queen said, "Good Hamlet, cast thy nighted color off."

The king said it showed good feeling to grieve for one's father but such grieving should not go on forever. Sooner or later, everyone's father died, and so it had been since the beginning of time. Hamlet should now begin to think of Claudius as his father.

Hamlet gave him one glance and looked away. Claudius went on. He hoped that Hamlet would not want to return to Wittenberg but would stay on in Denmark at Elsinore. The queen added, "Hamlet, I pray you to stay.,"

Hamlet bowed his head. "I will obey you, madam."

The king and queen seemed pleased enough by this to consider the conversation over. They rose, and in a noisy clatter of courtiers and attendants, they left the great hall.

All alone, Hamlet looked around the empty room, and then

down at his outstretched hands. At last he began to speak. "Oh, that this too too solid flesh would melt, thaw and resolve itself into dew!" he said. Life seemed weary, stale, flat, and unprofitable to him. He had believed in his mother's love for his father, a man very worthy of her love. Now, alone, he poured out his distress that she should have married her husband's brother so soon after her husband's death, especially when that brother was so inferior to her first husband.

Just then, Horatio and Marcellus came in, anxious to tell Hamlet about seeing his father's ghost the night before.

"You saw my father, the king?" said Hamlet. "Where? How?"

"Wait, and we will tell you all," said Horatio.

So then they told of seeing the ghost, armed from head to toe.

"Armed?" interrupted Hamlet.

Yes, they said. Head to toe.

"You are sure it was he?" asked Hamlet.

Yes, yes. They knew the looks of the old king.

Hamlet said, "I will watch tonight. Perhaps it will walk again. Perhaps speak."

"Good," said Horatio. "We will see you on the battlements between eleven and twelve." With that, he and Marcellus left, but now Hamlet had a new and strange suspicion. "My father armed? All is not well." He began to wonder if there had been foul play somewhere about which his father wanted to warn him.

Meantime, it seemed there was one person at Elsinore at whom Hamlet did smile, with whom he did exchange friendly words now and then. This was the pretty, gentle Ophelia, sister of Laertes and daughter of old Polonius.

Laertes, his trunks packed, ready for his trip to France, took some time to warn his sister against those friendly advances that

33

Hamlet made. She should not pay too much attention to them, he said. After all, Hamlet was going to be king of Denmark someday. It was not likely that he would be allowed to choose a bride for himself. "Be careful," said Laertes.

Ophelia was not too happy with this advice but before she could say much Polonius came in to say good-bye to his son.

Now it was Laertes's turn to get advice. Polonius launched into a lecture full of dos and don'ts. Laertes must be careful of his speech, never vulgar, true to real friends, careful about new acquaintances, and well-dressed but never gaudy. "Neither a borrower or a lender be, for loan oft loses both itself and friend," Polonius said and finally he wound up, "This above all, to thine own self be true, and it must follow as the night the day, thou canst not then be false to any man."

At last it was time for Laertes to go. He knelt for his father's blessing. Saying good-bye to Ophelia, he reminded her to heed his warnings. Then he was gone.

"So," said Polonius, "what was he warning you about?"

Ophelia answered honestly with the result that Polonius was launched on a new lecture. Ophelia tried to interrupt and tell him that Hamlet had made her an honorable proposal. But no, no, her father said. Hamlet was only amusing himself with her. She must promise him not to think of Hamlet as a suitor or to give him any more encouragement. Anything else would only lead to her own grief and disappointment. At last Ophelia bowed her head and promised.

As for Hamlet, just now he had his own concerns that had nothing to do with Ophelia. This was the night he was going to watch on the battlements for a sight of his father's ghost.

The torches sent flickering flares of light into the darkness when Hamlet joined Horatio and Marcellus. Horatio led the way to the spot where the ghost had appeared before. They stopped and spoke in hushed tones as they waited. And then, suddenly, there it was.

A misty figure, clad in armor from head to toe, just as Horatio had said, and now the spectre was beckoning to Hamlet to follow him.

All at once Horatio and Marcellus became frightened and tried to hold Hamlet back. Perhaps this was an evil spirit, a shade from hell, trying to lure Hamlet to his destruction. But Hamlet pushed them aside and followed the ghost down the battlement into the darkness where only the ghost seemed to glimmer with a dim brightness.

Then the ghost spoke. "I am your father's spirit," he said, "doomed for a certain time to walk the night." But then he said, "If ever thou didst love thy father, revenge his foul and unnatural murder!"

"Murder!" whispered Hamlet.

In quick, hushed tones, the ghost told the story. Everyone in Denmark had been told that he had met his death from the sting of a serpent while he was napping in the palace garden. True, a serpent had stung him, but that serpent now wore his crown.

"My uncle!" said Hamlet.

Yes, said the ghost, Hamlet's uncle, now married to Hamlet's mother. What had really happened was that as the king lay napping, his brother had slipped up on him and poured poison in his ears, a poison so violent that death was almost instant.

"O, horrible, O, horrible, most horrible," said the ghost. "If thou hast nature in thee bear it not…"

But now a faint glow of dawn showed in the sky. The ghost must leave. "Adieu, Hamlet, remember me," he said and vanished.

Hamlet stood for a moment, trying to take in all he had heard. Then he vowed to the ghost of his father that he would indeed remember—and avenge him.

Vaguely he heard the worried voices of Horatio and Marcellus calling him. Soon they joined him and were asking what had happened. Hamlet shook his head and would say nothing in particular. But he did make them swear that they would tell no one what they had seen that night.

"Swear!" he said, and a ghostly voice from somewhere echoed, "Swear!" Quickly and fearfully, his friends swore as he asked them. Then they turned to leave the battlement.

"Rest, rest, perturbed spirit," said Hamlet softly to the vanished ghost, but then he muttered, "The time is out of joint. O, cursed spite, that ever I was born to set it right."

He had seen. He had heard. As he had guessed, there was "something rotten in the state of Denmark." His uncle had not only married his mother in undue haste but he had first of all murdered his father. And Hamlet had sworn he would avenge those acts.

But suddenly it was not all that easy. Hamlet became tormented with doubts. Was it really his father's ghost he had seen? Was his uncle really a murderer? He began to act in a distracted manner as the days went by. Before, he had been silent. Now he talked, but in such a confusing way that no one understood him.

One day he frightened Ophelia by running into her sewing room, his doublet all unbuttoned, and kneeling down before her. He took her face in his hands, stared in her eyes for a moment, sighed, and then rushed away again.

When Ophelia told her father about this, Polonius now decided he had been wrong in thinking Hamlet was trifling with his daughter. He had been wrong too in telling her to rebuff him. Hamlet's strange behavior all stemmed from the fact that he was mad with love.

The king and queen, also troubled by Hamlet's behavior, had summoned two of his childhood friends, Rosencrantz and Guildenstern, to Elsinore. These were two amiable fellows who were happy to agree to the king's request—that they spend some time with Hamlet and try to discover the cause of his erratic behavior. They wandered off to search for their old friend just as Polonius came hurrying in, bursting with news. He had received word from Norway that the king's letters, urging peace, had been well-received. It seemed unlikely that young Fortinbras would try any invasion of Denmark. But even more important, Polonius was sure he knew what was wrong with Hamlet. He was in love with Ophelia and gone a little crazy because she rebuffed him.

The king and queen wondered. Could that really be the answer? Polonius said he could prove it. Just let him speak to Hamlet in the long hall, where he sometimes went to read, or any place, and he would soon have the truth from him. Polonius now hurried off to begin a program of spying on Hamlet and popping out whenever it seemed he might surprise him into some revelation.

He had just popped out on Hamlet in the long hall and after a few words with him decided there was "method in his madness," when Rosencrantz and Guildenstern appeared. Polonius left and Hamlet was happy to greet his old friends. But even from them he could not conceal his melancholy. "Man delights not me; no, nor woman neither..."

His friends were sorry to hear this. Among other things it meant that he would not be pleased to hear that a company of strolling players was on its way to the castle, hoping to be asked to put on some sort of entertainment.

To their surprise, Hamlet seemed interested. He was more than interested. An idea had come to him of how he might resolve some of the doubts that were distracting him.

Just then, with some flourishes on a horn, the players arrived, escorted by Polonius. Hamlet greeted them warmly, told Polonius to see they were well fed and accommodated. But he asked the chief player to stay a moment. He asked the actor if he knew the play about the murder of Gonzago. Of course, said the actor. Well, could he put it on tomorrow night, asked Hamlet, and could he add some dialogue which Hamlet would write? Of course, said the actor, nothing easier. Ah, said Hamlet, very good.

Then he sent the actor off with Rosencrantz and Guildenstern to follow Polonius and the others. And as so often, what he could not say to others, he began to voice aloud to himself. He was ashamed that he was so slow in taking vengeance for his father. Why did he need more proof? Still, he had heard that sometimes guilty people viewing a play were struck by some resemblance to their own acts and made some move that betrayed it. He would have the players put on a drama something like the murder of his father and observe his uncle's looks. "If he but blench, I know my course... The play's the thing wherein I'll catch the conscience of the king."

Next day Polonius had Ophelia with him as he came for his audience with the king. The king was already talking to Rosencrantz and Guildenstern. Had they learned anything about what distressed Hamlet, he asked. No, they said, not really. But he had seemed pleased that the players were going to put on a performance this evening and hoped that the king and queen would be there. They promised they would be and the two young men left.

Now the king asked the queen to leave also. Polonius had a new scheme. He and Polonius were going to hide while Ophelia sat in a corner reading. Hamlet had been summoned, and from their hiding places they would see how he behaved with her.

The king and Polonius hid themselves. Ophelia took out her book and sat in her corner and soon Hamlet came in. Thinking himself alone, he began to speak his thoughts—once more about suicide. "To be or not to be," he wondered aloud. "To die, to sleep; to sleep, perchance to dream; ay, there's the rub..." And so he pondered the question, thinking "conscience doth make cowards of us all."

And then he saw Ophelia.

It was not a happy meeting.

She offered to return the gifts he had given her. He swore he had never given her any gifts, but he did say he had loved her once.

"My lord, you made me believe so."

She should not have believed him, said Hamlet. Now his advice to her was to get to a nunnery. She tried to reason with him. He wanted none of it. "Get thee to a nunnery, go," he said and walked away.

In due time, the king and Polonius came out from their hiding places. Polonius still thought Hamlet's wild words were caused by unrequited love but the king was less and less sure. Something stranger and heavier seemed to be brooding on his spirit. Perhaps, the king said, it might be a good idea to send Hamlet away from Denmark for a while. Perhaps to England.

But that night there was the play. The king and queen took their places. All the members of the court arranged themselves around them. Hamlet decided to loll at Ophelia's feet and tease her, but his eyes were constantly on his uncle as the actors began their play.

The play began with a king and queen walking in a garden and the queen swearing undying love for the king. Even if he were to die she would never marry again. Then she left the king as he went to sleep for a while. Then in came the king's nephew, looking about him furtively, stealing up on the sleeping king and then opening a vial and pouring some fluid in his ears.

A chair scraped loudly. King Claudius was on his feet. "Lights, lights!" cried the courtiers around the king and some servants quickly lighted torches.

It was plain that the play had not pleased the king. In no time, he and the queen and all their attendants had left. Hamlet and Horatio were alone. Hamlet asked if Horatio had noticed the king's reaction to the poisoning scene. Indeed he had.

Before they could say more, Guildenstern came in to tell Hamlet that the king seemed in a troubled mood and that his mother wanted to see him in her chambers. Hamlet nodded but did not hurry off. Instead, he began teasing Guildenstern, accusing him of spying on him. Then Polonius hurried in, also bearing the message that the queen wanted to see Hamlet. Hamlet teased him for a bit too, before he sent everyone away so he could brood a little about what he would say to his mother.

While he brooded, the king was indeed troubled and was arranging with Rosencrantz and Guildenstern to go with Hamlet to England for a while. When they left, Polonius was at the king's elbow, saying he was going to hide behind the tapestry in the queen's bedroom to hear what she and Hamlet had to say. Finally alone, the king seemed to feel a rare agony of spirit. He went to a small altar in an alcove and knelt before it, murmuring of his guilt and wishing he could properly repent.

Hamlet saw him there on his knees as he was going to his mother's room and his hand moved toward his dagger. How easy it would be to kill Claudius now and avenge his father. But no. He would not kill him while he was praying, his sins confessed, his soul free for heaven. He moved quietly away and finally made his way to his mother's room, knocked, and entered.

"Hamlet," she said, "you have much offended your father."

"Mother," he said "you have much offended my father."

He was determined to make her see how she had erred in marrying her husband's brother. He wanted her to look at herself as she was. He pushed a mirror before her.

"Help," she cried, "help."

A voice from behind the tapestry cried, "What ho! Help! Help!"

In an instant, Hamlet swung and plunged his dagger into a bulging shape behind the tapestry.

"Ohh!" came a cry from the tapestry, and then the sound of a body falling. "I am slain."

Hamlet drew back the tapestry and there lay old Polonius, at last caught in his spying. "Alas, poor fool, I took thee for thy better," said Hamlet. Then he turned from the dead man to his distracted mother. He might have killed Polonius but still he was determined to make his mother admit her shame and guilt.

As he pleaded with her it seemed he saw again his father's ghost, urging him on. His mother by now was convinced Hamlet was totally mad. Her one objective was to calm him until finally he said good night and departed, dragging Polonius's body with him.

Hamlet's killing of Polonius had convinced the king that no time must be lost in getting him out of Denmark. Next morning he told Rosencrantz and Guildenstern that a ship would be ready that afternoon to take them and Hamlet to England. Later the king told Hamlet he feared there would be such an outcry at the death of Polonius that it would be better for him to go to England. Hamlet nodded, making no objection, and went to prepare for the journey.

Only after Hamlet and the two young men had said their good-byes and were on their way, did the king rub his hands together, congratulating himself. He had given Rosencrantz and Guildenstern a letter to the English king, asking not sanctuary for Hamlet, but his death.

But Hamlet's departure brought no peace to the troubled palace of Elsinore. He had hardly been gone a day or two when the gentle Ophelia was trailing through its halls, her hair undone, her eyes blank, as she sang one sorrowful ditty after another.

The king was sure it was the shock of her father's death that had upset her sanity. "Good night ladies, good night, sweet ladies," she sang as she trailed away.

But there was no time to brood about her problem for now there was a tumult at the doors and in came Laertes, back from France, with a crowd of Danes behind him. He had heard of his father's murder and of how the king had quickly and quietly buried him. He had come for vengeance.

The king was trying to assure him that the deed had not been his when Ophelia walked in again, as distracted as before.

Laertes stared, astounded, as she sang her little songs and then began throwing flowers and herbs before her. "There's rosemary, that's for remembrance; pray, love remember . . ."

"Do you see this, O God?" cried Laertes.

The king tried to calm him, saying that her sorrow too would be avenged.

Meantime, by a strange set of circumstances, Hamlet was back in Denmark. The ship on which he and his companions had set sail had been overtaken by pirates but only he, Hamlet, had been taken off the ship by the pirates, and later, put ashore in Denmark.

Horatio had the news first, in a letter brought by some sailors, and in the letter Hamlet had fixed a time and place for their meeting. Then the king was brought a letter. He told Laertes the astonishing news. Hamlet was on his way to Elsinore.

"Let him come!" cried Laertes, gripping his dagger.

But King Claudius had a better plan. Laertes was known as a fine swordsman. Let him challenge Hamlet to a duel in the course of which he could surely run him through with no blame attached.

"Aha!" said Laertes, and he had a further idea. He had some poison with which he could smear the tip of his sword so there would be no doubt of the outcome. Splendid, said the king, and he added another refinement. There would be wine on hand for the duelists to drink to refresh themselves. He would see to it that one cup was poisoned.

Then in came the queen, wringing her hands. "One woe comes upon another's heels . . . Your sister's drowned, Laertes."

"Drowned? Where? How?"

Now the queen told the pitiful story of how the deranged maiden had crowned herself with flowers and laid down in the stream which had floated her gently for a while, but then sucked her under to her death.

"Drowned," said Laertes again, and the king hoped he would be able to keep Laertes calm enough to settle the score with Hamlet in the duel as planned.

Hamlet and Horatio met as planned and were passing the churchyard on their way to Elsinore. They saw some grave-diggers digging a new grave and stopped to watch. The grave-diggers were untroubled by their work and threw out bones as they came to them. They threw a skull, which landed at Hamlet's feet, saying cheerfully that it had been Yorick, the king's jester.

Hamlet picked up the skull and pondered it. "Alas, poor Yorick! I knew him, Horatio, a fellow of infinite jest, of most excellent fancy . . ."

The funeral procession making for the grave now came their way. There was the bier on which lay Ophelia, and behind it came the priests, Laertes, the king and queen, and some of their attendants.

As they came to the open grave Laertes was complaining that the services had been cut short. The priest answered that for anyone who had died as Ophelia had, that was all the church allowed.

"Ophelia? The fair Ophelia?" cried Hamlet. And then, as Laertes jumped into the grave in some paroxysm of grief, Hamlet jumped in after him. Only face-to-face in the grave did they recognize each other. Laertes grabbed at once for Hamlet's throat.

It took a bit of doing to separate the two but the king was determined and finally the funeral was properly concluded.

Back at the palace, Hamlet told Horatio of finding the letter the king had sent to England with Rosencrantz and Guildenstern, ordering his death and of how he had substituted another for it, ordering their death instead. Horatio said the king will find out soon enough. Yes, said Hamlet, but the interim is mine, and a man's life is no more than to say "one."

Word came from the great hall that everything was ready for the fencing match with Laertes. Was Hamlet ready? "If it be now," he said, "'tis not to come; if it be not to come, it will be now . . . the readiness is all."

He went into the great hall and now he offered Laertes his apologies for everything he had done in his madness. Then they took up their foils and began to fence. The king carefully set out the cups of wine, one of which he had poisoned for Hamlet.

Flick, flick, the swords touched and flashed and parried and darted and touched again.

"A hit! A very palpable hit!" said Hamlet at one point.

"Stay!" said the king. "have a drink now," and he held out the poisoned cup.

"Not just now," said Hamlet. "Set it by for a while," and he and Laertes began to fence again.

The queen reached for the cup that the king had set by and lifted it to her lips. "No," cried the king, but he was too late. She had already drunk from it.

And now Hamlet was wounded by Laertes's rapier. They were scuffling, and in the scuffle they dropped their swords, and by chance each picked up the other's weapon. Then Hamlet had wounded Laertes with the poisoned sword.

The queen was rising, clutching her throat. She fell to the ground. "The drink, the drink, dear Hamlet," she whispered as she died.

Feeling the venom in his wound, Laertes confessed to Hamlet about the poisoned sword and the poisoned cup, which was the king's doing.

"Ah," said Hamlet as he ran to the king and stabbed him, "venom do thy work." Soon the king was dying; so was Laertes. The queen was dead and now Hamlet was dying too.

Horatio picked up the poisoned cup and would have drunk from it himself to join Hamlet, but Hamlet whispered no. "In this harsh world, draw thy breath awhile to tell my story."

Then Hamlet too was dead.

Looking down on him, Horatio said, "Now cracks a noble heart. Good night, sweet prince, and flights of angels sing thee to thy rest."

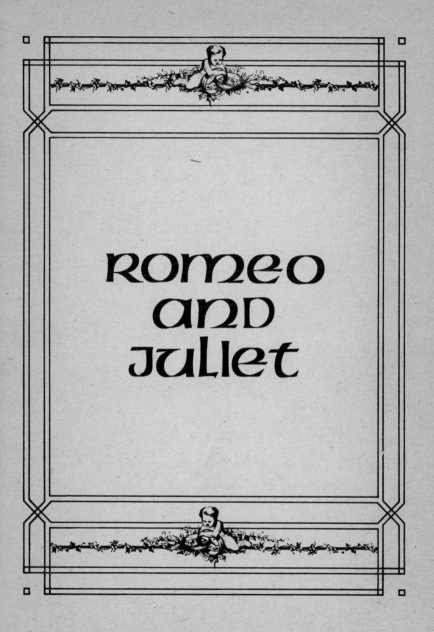

ROMEO
AND
JULIET

I F ONLY there had not been the feu... ing young people of Verona might have ... with all proper ceremony and lived happy an... ...perous lives together.

But there was the feud. Between the families Capulet and Montague. No one remembered any longer how it had started. But so violent was the feeling that friends of the Capulets fought friends of the Montagues when they met in the street. Servants of the Montagues brawled with the servants of the Capulets in the marketplace.

One day Tybalt, a hot-headed nephew of Lady Capulet, had managed to pick a fight with Benvolio, who was of the Montague family, when the Prince of Verona appeared on the scene.

"Enough!" cried the Prince. "This quarrel between Montague and Capulet has disturbed our city long enough. Now it must end. If there is any more of it, those involved will forfeit with their lives." He arranged to meet with Lord Montague and Lord Capulet in his chambers to make sure they understood and would enforce his ban.

Young Romeo, son and heir of the Montagues, did not pay much attention to the feud anyway. His thoughts were mostly of romance. He was mooning along the street, dreaming of the latest charmer who had caught his eye, when Benvolio fell into step beside him.

Benvolio asked who it was now and when Romeo sighed and answered, "Rosaline," he laughed. Romeo knew nothing about love yet, he said. He was just playing with dreams of romance.

Meantime, Lord Capulet was walking down another street with Paris, a young nobleman and kinsman of the prince. He talked of the ban on the feud. "It should not be hard to keep the peace," he said. "We are both old men, Montague and I. Why do we need to fight?"

Paris nodded but he had something else on his mind. He wanted to talk to Lord Capulet about Juliet, Capulet's only daughter and the apple of his eye. Paris asked if he might court her.

"She is very young," answered Capulet, "not quite fourteen. However, you have my permission to woo her and if you win her heart, I will consent. You will have a chance to try your luck tonight for I am giving a ball, inviting friends from all over the city. Ho!" he called, summoning his servant, who was trudging along behind.

"Here," he said, and handed him a list of names. "Go and summon all these friends of mine to feasting and dancing at my home tonight."

Perhaps he had forgotten that the servant could not read. He and Paris went off down the street, leaving the servant staring at the list.

When Romeo and Benvolio came along, still arguing about love, the servant begged a favor. "Sir, can you read?"

So it came about that Romeo Montague read off the whole guest list for the Capulet feast and in no time he and Benvolio had decided to attend it. "I'll show you some real beauties tonight," said Benvolio, "then compare your Rosaline to them."

Preparations for the party at the Capulet house were all completed that evening when Juliet's old nurse went to Juliet's room calling for her. Her mother, Lady Capulet, wanted to see her. Juliet came running in from the balcony as her mother entered. Lady Capulet looked at her daughter, slender and lovely and no longer a child. She smoothed the girl's hair, redid a ribbon on her dress, and said, "Yes, it's time to think of marriage now. And brave Paris has asked for your love."

"Ah, Paris!" cried the nurse. "There's a man."

"Tonight you can study him at the feast," said Lady Capulet.

"See if you do not find him worthy of your love."

Juliet smiled. "I will look at him, of course, and see what I see. I cannot say more."

Just then a servant came in to announce that the feast was all ready. Guests were waiting. It was time for them to go downstairs.

Romeo, Benvolio, and another friend, Mercutio, lingered outside the Capulet house until the dining was over. They thought it would be easier to mingle with the guests when they were dancing and not be detected as Montagues. Even so, Romeo felt a little apprehensive as he entered the house of the longtime enemies of his family.

But once inside there was all the happy roar of a good party. Musicians were fiddling and young people were dancing. Around the walls, the older folk sat and watched and chatted.

And then it happened. Romeo saw Juliet and she saw him. They were almost a room apart from each other but that did not matter. Their eyes were fixed on each other.

> "O, she doth teach the torches to burn bright!
> It seems she hangs upon the cheek of night
> Like a rich jewel in an Ethiope's ear;
> Beauty too rich for use, for earth too dear."

Every love Romeo had imagined before was forgotten. He knew he had never seen real beauty before.

Unfortunately, the quarrelsome Tybalt was nearby. He recognized Romeo Montague and drew his rapier.

"What's this?" called Lord Capulet, who saw the move.

"Uncle, this is a Montague come to mock us," said Tybalt.

"Never mind," called his uncle. "There will be no fighting here tonight. Put away your sword."

"Ah, it's too bad," grumbled Tybalt as he stamped out of the

51

ballroom, cheated of a fight.

The two young people had not heard a word of this. Step by step they had moved closer to each other till their hands were touching. They were speaking softly to each other.

The old nurse broke the spell. "Madam," she said, bustling up to Juliet, "your mother wants a word with you." Obediently, Juliet turned to go to her mother but her eyes lingered on Romeo.

Still in a daze, Romeo asked, "Who is her mother?"

"Why, sure, her mother is the lady of the house," said the nurse.

"A Capulet?" Romeo asked. "O, my life is my foe's debt…"

A few minutes later Juliet was discovering that the young man who had won her heart at first sight was a Montague. "O," she cried, "o, my only love sprung from my only hate…Prodigious birth of love it is to me that I must love a loathed enemy…"

Enemy, they both whispered to themselves; foe. And then they brushed the words aside. They had no meaning anymore.

The ball was over. It was late at night, or perhaps early morning. Romeo stood by the wall that surrounded the Capulet house and then jumped over it and walked through the orchard toward the house. He saw a figure appear at the lighted door on the upper story and then slip out onto the balcony. Was it— could it be? It was. "It is the east, and Juliet is the sun," Romeo whispered. He came nearer and watched as she leaned on the balcony railing. "O, that I were a glove upon that hand, that I might touch that cheek."

Juliet sighed, "Ah me."

"She speaks!" he said. "O, speak again, bright angel."

Juliet began talking to herself. "O, Romeo, Romeo, wherefore art thou Romeo? Deny thy father and refuse thy name; or, if thou wilt not, be but sworn my love, and I'll no longer be a

Capulet."

Romeo came nearer. It was time to let her know he was there. "Call me but love," he said, "and I'll be new baptized."

Juliet started. Who was there? But she knew, really.

How had he gotten there? she asked. The wall was so high. Besides, it was dangerous. If any of her kinsmen found him they would surely kill him.

Romeo scoffed at that. He was hidden by the night. Now Juliet remembered the words of love she had spoken when she thought she was alone. She was embarrassed for a moment. Then she put such thoughts aside to ask Romeo if he loved her.

"Lady, by yonder blessed moon I swear," he began.

But she interrupted. "O, swear not by the moon, the inconstant moon...."

"Then what?"

"O, do not swear at all but by thy gracious self."

And now they began a murmuring of their love that was like music on the night air, like honey, like the fluttering of bird's wings. Once and again, Juliet's nurse called to her. Juliet slipped in to answer her and then hurried back.

It was all magical, so sudden it was almost frightening. But no, not really. Juliet was telling Romeo that she would marry him on the coming day if he so wished. He did wish. Very well. Juliet would send a messenger to him and he would give the messenger full particulars of where and at what time they should meet.

Again the nurse called. Juliet ran in and then out again. It really was time for Romeo to go. But first they agreed on nine o'clock as the hour when Juliet should send her messenger. Then they had to speak again about the wonder of their love. Until finally Juliet was whispering, "Good night, good night! Parting is such sweet sorrow that I shall say good night till it be morrow." Then she dashed inside and closed the door.

Friar Laurence was a gentle old man who liked to gather herbs in the fields outside the cell where he lived and then prepare them into healing potions. He was out in front of his cell this morning with his basket, pondering on the mystery of why some herbs should have poisonous qualities as well as healing ones, when Romeo came up.

The old man was astonished to see Romeo at such an early hour. Had he stayed up all night? With Rosaline?

Romeo shook his head. No, no. Rosaline was forgotten. Something wonderful had happened. He had found his heart's true love—Juliet of the Capulets. He wanted the friar to marry them this afternoon.

The friar blinked at such haste and had to remind Romeo of how he had sighed over Rosaline. Was he really sure this new love was different? Finally Romeo convinced him and the friar nodded. Juliet was a far different girl from Rosaline. He would perform the marriage this afternoon in his cell, and perhaps this marriage might help seal the breach between the feuding families.

Eagerly, Romeo hurried to the center of town to wait for the messenger Juliet would be sending. His two friends, Benvolio and Mercutio, were near the square, pondering a challenge that Tybalt, that fiery Capulet, had sent to Romeo. But when Romeo joined them their talk turned to jokes and teasing about where he had been the night before.

Then Juliet's nurse came shuffling down the street and Romeo left them to question her. Did she come from her mistress? The nurse was a born talker, but at last she admitted that she did. Romeo gave her his message. Juliet was to be at Friar Laurence's cell that afternoon. Meantime, the nurse was to pick up a rope ladder from Romeo's servant and hide it near Juliet's balcony so he could mount to her room that night.

"O nurse, sweet nurse, what news?" Juliet cried as the nurse came shuffling back. "Tell me, what says my love?" Finally she got it out of her. The friar's cell that afternoon. Romeo would be waiting.

And so he was, along with Friar Laurence who was again cautioning him about being too impetuous. "These violent delights have violent ends," he said somberly. But there came Juliet, and the lovers had no more interest in advice. They were holding hands before the old friar. He was marrying them.

After that Juliet had to flee back home. But Romeo would be coming that night to climb the ladder to her room. She had only to wait, counting the minutes.

Alas that Romeo wandered off to the square to while away his hours that hot afternoon. Benvolio and Mercutio were still there but now came Tybalt, spoiling for a fight.

"Aha! there's my man," he cried when he saw Romeo. "There's the villain."

Romeo tried to calm him, saying he had never done him any injury and now in fact he had reasons to love him.

This was nonsense to Tybalt. He hated Romeo because he hated him.

Suddenly, Mercutio had had enough. He drew his sword. "Step forward," he said.

Tybalt was more than ready, lifting his sword to parry and thrust.

"No, no," cried Romeo. "Mercutio, put up your sword. Have you forgotten the prince's ruling?"

But now the swords were flashing.

"Stop!" Romeo cried. "Benvolio, beat down their swords." Then, in an effort to separate the duelists, Romeo stepped between them just as Tybalt made a mighty lunge. His sword passed under Romeo's arm and into Mercutio's body.

Mercutio fell, crying, "I am hurt." Tybalt ran off and Romeo bent, horrified, over Mercutio. "Courage, man, the hurt cannot be much."

Mercutio groaned. "No, 'tis not so deep as a well, not so wide as a church-door, but 'tis enough, 'twill serve...I was hurt under your arm. Why did you come between us?"

Why? Romeo had thought he was helping.

"Help me into some house, Benvolio," Mercutio whispered. And now, as Benvolio did so, Romeo stood desolate, thinking that his good friend might have taken mortal hurt for defending Romeo.

All too soon Benvolio was back to say that Mercutio was dead. And then Tybalt came swinging down the street again. The sight of him was too much for Romeo. He pulled his sword from its sheath and ran at Tybalt crying, "You or I!"

They fought in a frenzy and then in a flash Romeo had a lucky stroke. Tybalt fell at his feet.

Benvolio was gasping in horror. "Run, Romeo. Run and hide." A crowd of people was gathering. "Run. You know the prince will doom you if you are taken." Romeo darted off.

It was none too soon. The crowd collected around Tybalt's body, crying out and lamenting. The prince himself appeared and demanded to know who had committed this new outrage. When he learned it was Romeo Montague, he pronounced his judgment. Romeo was banished from Verona from that day on.

The old nurse brought the news to Juliet and garbled it so that at first Juliet thought Romeo was dead. She cried out in relief when she heard that was not so but she was half sick to know that her gentle husband had killed her cousin. And now he was banished. What a wedding day—and oh, what a woeful wedding night.

Now, now, her nurse soothed her. She was sure she knew where Romeo would be hiding. There was still the rope ladder by which he could climb to her balcony.

For once, the old nurse managed an errand fairly quickly. She found Romeo at Friar Laurence's cell, as she had expected, and told him that Juliet would be waiting for him that night.

And so when dark had truly fallen, Romeo stole out and made his way secretly to the Capulet house, over the wall, and up the ladder. Then he and Juliet were in each other's arms.

The night of love went all too quickly. The gray dawn came and they tried to reassure each other that this parting would not be forever. Romeo would go to Mantua and soon he would find a way to send for Juliet. But oh, the sorrow of parting. One kiss and then one more. Then he slipped down the ladder.

He was barely gone when Lady Capulet knocked and came in. She saw tears on Juliet's cheeks and thought she was crying for the death of her cousin, Tybalt. She had a few grim words to say about Romeo who had killed him and how she might send an assassin after him to Mantua. "O, mother, that I might be that one," said Juliet.

"Never mind. I'll find someone," said her mother. But now she had more surprising news. "Your father has found a husband for you, the gallant young nobleman, Paris. You will be married this Thursday at Saint Peter's Church."

Juliet stared at her mother. "I pray you tell my lord and father, madam, I will not marry yet; and when I do, I swear it shall be Romeo, whom you know I hate, rather than Paris."

Lady Capulet was not pleased by this response. "Very well. Here comes your father. You tell him that and see how he takes it."

Lord Capulet came in along with the nurse, and he too saw that Juliet had been weeping. He too thought it was for Tybalt.

Then Lady Capulet told him that Juliet was not willing to marry Paris.

"What? What's that? Not willing? What sort of child is this?" Soon he had worked himself into a terrible temper. Juliet was weeping again and on her knees before him.

"Please, father, please, I beg you, I cannot."

Her tears, her pleas were of no use. Capulet's voice was cold, his eyes angry. "Be at that church on Thursday morning or you are no more child of mine," he said and stomped out.

Juliet ventured one more plea to her mother but she too turned her back. "I have done with you," she said, and left the room.

"O nurse, nurse, what am I going to do?" sobbed Juliet.

What she did, before too long, was dress herself and make her way to Friar Laurence's cell. He already knew of her father's plans for her because Paris had been there asking him to perform the marriage ceremony.

Now Juliet was weeping again as she asked if her only way out of her difficulties was to kill herself.

The old friar shook his head and seemed lost in thought. At last he began to speak slowly of a rare herbal concoction he had brewed. It was a desperate remedy but if she dared—

"O, tell me," she cried.

"It is a liquor that brings on the very look of death for forty-two hours. You drink it and a drowsy numbness comes over you, and then, gradually, a deep slumber that all around you will mistake for death. If you dare it, this would be the plan. You will go home and pretend to agree with your father's plans. You will be the good, obedient daughter of old. When you go to bed Wednesday night, sleep alone, without your nurse in the room. Drink the potion. By morning, when they come to wake you the spell will be in full effect. They will think you dead. Then, as is the custom here, before too long they will bear you to the vault where all the Capulets lie. Meantime, I shall have sent for Romeo and together he and I will watch for your awakening. Then he will carry you off with him to Mantua. Have you the strength for this?"

Juliet said, "O, give me, give me, and do not talk to me of fear."

Her parents, of course, were delighted by her change in mood, and bustled about with preparations for the wedding on Thursday. All through Wednesday, the happy fuss went on. At night, Juliet said loving good nights to her parents and her nurse and closed the door of her bedroom.

Alone on her bed, holding the little vial the friar had given her, she could not help but feel some fear. What if the old friar had made some mistake in the concoction and brewed poison? What if she woke alone in the vault and saw ghosts of her ancestors—or of Tybalt?

She summoned all her courage; opened the vial, and lifted it to her lips.

"Romeo, I come! this do I drink to thee!"

Oh, the outcry that next morning in the Capulet household when Juliet was discovered, pale and pulseless on her bed. The nurse shrieked, Lady Capulet moaned; Capulet, on the other hand, was stunned into silence. Friar Laurence arrived with Paris, the prospective bridegroom, and there was more shock and lamentation. At the same time, Friar Laurence was quietly urging that the dead girl be taken to the Capulet vault as soon as possible.

The gay white decorations for the wedding were put aside. The musicians were sent away. Black hangings covered the bier as the sad procession made its way to the tomb. The heavy iron cover was lifted. Juliet was carried down the stone steps and laid on a sepulchre. Then the weeping group bade her farewell and went up the steps and closed the cover again.

In Mantua, Romeo waited for a message from Friar Laurence. When he saw his servant, Balshassar, come riding up, he greeted him eagerly. What was the news from Verona? How was Juliet? Did he have a letter from Friar Laurence?

No, said Balshassar, he had no letter from the friar. As for Juliet… He took a while to tell it. Juliet was dead.

Dead? Romeo could not believe it. Then he fell into a perfect frenzy. He must have a horse at once. No, first he must go to a little apothecary he knew and get a vial of poison. Poison, a horse—soon he and Balshassar were on their way.

Night had fallen when they arrived at Verona but a few torches were flaring in the graveyard. Romeo did not stop to wonder who held them or why. His one concern was to get his own torch lighted. Then he told Balshassar he had no more need for him and ran toward the tomb. He set the torch in the ground as he moved the heavy cover and was about to go down the stone steps when someone stepped forward out of the dark. It was Paris who had come to grieve at Juliet's tomb, and now recognized Romeo. To Paris, Romeo was simply Tybalt's killer, whose death had caused Juliet to cry so much.

"Halt, vile Montague," Paris said. "Stop whatever unhallowed task you come for. Obey and come with me, for you must die."

Romeo did not recognize Paris. "Yes, I must indeed," he answered, "and for that I came hither. And now, good gentle youth, fly from here. Do not tempt a desperate man."

But Paris would not be put off. He was determined to bring Romeo to justice. In no time, they had drawn their swords. Romeo's desperate sword flashed the fastest. Paris fell. "I am slain," he whispered. "If you are merciful, put me in the tomb with Juliet."

Now Romeo did recognize Paris and recalled some talk of Balshassar's on their wild ride to Verona. Something about Paris wanting to marry Juliet? Or had he dreamed it? He lifted Paris's body and carried it down into the tomb and laid it on a sepulchre. Then he turned to the still figure of Juliet.

"O, my love! my wife!" he cried. He stared at her and felt that death had no power over her beauty. He knelt beside her, promising he would never leave her.

"Eyes, look your last," he whispered. "Arms, take your last embrace." Then he took the vial of poison from his belt and lifted it to his lips. "Here's to my love!"

He drank the poison and almost at once fell forward. "O, true apothecary! Thy drugs are quick. Thus with a kiss I die."

Meantime, Friar Laurence had learned that his letter to Romeo in Mantua had not been delivered. He worried about that but knew it was almost time for Juliet to awake from her drugged sleep. He hurried from his cell to the graveyard and there he was met with one surprise and horror after another. Paris's servants told him they were waiting for the arrival of the night watch which one of them had summoned. But why? Then he saw the blood of the stone steps of the tomb. Something awful had happened. He went down into the tomb and saw Romeo, lying beside Juliet's bier. He saw Paris, dead, on another sepulchre.

Just then Juliet began to waken from her long sleep. She blinked and saw the friar and smiled. "O, comfortable friar, where is my Romeo?"

The friar was distracted. "O, lady, a greater power than we can contradict has thwarted our intents. Come, come, you must away from here. Your husband is dead and Paris too... I will take you to a sisterhood of holy nuns..."

Shouting outside the tomb further unnerved him. "Come, it is the watch. We must go." And he hurried away, thinking she would follow. But Juliet was gazing at Romeo, then looking at the vial of poison still in his hand. "O, churl," she whispered, "drunk all, and left no friendly drop to help me after." She kissed him, hoping a drop of poison lingered on his lips. Then she saw the dagger at his belt.

"O, happy dagger!" she said, drawing it from the belt. "This is thy sheath," and she stabbed herself and fell on Romeo's body.

Too late, the men of the night watch came shouting and halloing into the churchyard and then the tomb.

Too late, Capulets and Montagues alike met in the tomb where their children both lay dead. Now they heard the whole story of the secret marriage from Friar Laurence, and weeping for the tragedies their long quarrel had caused, swore an end to it and to friendship in the future.

The Prince of Verona, who came along with the watch at the general alarm, looked on at this belated truce. Friendship now was of no help to these lovers, and it was a sad morning:

> "For never was a story of more woe
> Than this of Juliet and her Romeo."

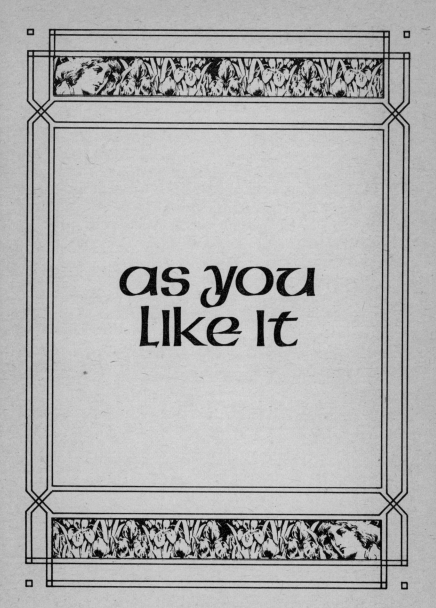

as you
Like It

I T ALL HAPPENED in the springtime—the green and flowery springtime—in a little kingdom ruled, at the moment, by a bad-tempered duke named Ferdinand.

What happened first—at least as far as this story goes—was that a young man named Orlando finally convinced his older brother, Oliver, to give him his share of their father's inheritance, so that he could go out in the world on his own. "On your own to throw it all away, one way or another," sneered Oliver, for he was bad-tempered also.

Orlando hoped that would not happen. All that he had in mind at present was a visit to the duke's palace to challenge the duke's famous wrestler, Charles, to a match, for Orlando thought himself fairly good at the sport.

Oliver, of course, thought he was a fool to challenge the duke's wrestler. He did not know why he resented his handsome younger brother so much. He just wished that when the wrestler took him on he would break his neck.

The next day, a good many people were gathered on the lawns of the duke's palace to watch the wrestling. But over on a green bank, two young girls were deep in a conversation of their own. One of them, Celia, was Duke Ferdinand's daughter. The other, her cousin and best friend, was Rosalind. And just to complicate things, she was the daughter of Duke Ferdinand's older brother, whom he had deposed and banished.

"I pray thee, Rosalind, sweet my coz, be merry," begged Celia. True, Celia's father had taken over all of Rosalind's father's lands and possessions and Rosalind stayed on at the palace only because Celia insisted on it. But, said Celia, what her father now possessed would one day be hers, and once hers, it would be Rosalind's. "So let us be merry," said Celia.

Rosalind cheered up and said very well, it might be good

sport to fall in love. Oh, no, said Celia. Let's not fool around with that.

The clown, Touchstone, came rollicking up and teased them for a while, and then M. Le Beau, the palace busybody, came to tell them that the next wrestling match was to take place just in front of them. Unless thay wanted to see some breaking of ribs they had better leave.

"Leave? But why?" they said. Just then, along came Charles, the duke's wrestler, and beside him, young Orlando, and following them, the duke and a whole train of spectators.

The girls' eyes were all for the young man. *He* was the one who was challenging Charles? Oh, no. What a shame for his ribs to be broken. They ran down the bank to him.

"Please," they said. "Do you really want to wrestle with *him?*" They looked fearfully toward Charles, who was flexing his great muscles and then back to Orlando. "O, for your own sake, give over this attempt."

Orlando smiled at them and said that though he hated to deny them anything, this was a contest he had chosen to enter.

"Come on, come on," roared the wrestler.

"Just wish me well," said Orlando and both girls said that yes, yes, of course they did.

He moved toward the big wrestler and they began to lunge, grab at each other, and reach for holds. Suddenly, Orlando lifted his opponent and threw him to the ground, knocking the wind out of him.

Celia and Rosalind were delighted. "O, good," they cried, "o, splendid."

The duke was not so pleased. At first he wanted the fight to go on, but when it was clear that Charles was in no shape for that, he called Orlando to him. He asked his name. Orlando told him, adding that he was the younger son of Sir Rowland de

Boys. At this the duke frowned.

"I would it had been another," said the duke. "The world knew him as an honorable man but we were never friends. Well, you put up a gallant fight even so."

With that, the duke left for the palace, trailed by his attendants. This gave Celia and Rosalind a chance to run up to Orlando and congratulate him. On an impulse, Rosalind took off the chain she was wearing and put it around Orlando's neck.

"And to think," said Rosalind, "that your father was Sir Roland de Boys. He was my father's dearest friend."

"Really?" said Orlando. And he and Rosalind stared at each other as though this were the most wonderful coincidence that had ever happened.

When Celia finally pulled Rosalind away toward the palace, Orlando stood staring after them in a daze. M. Le Beau, bustling as usual, came up to tell them that the duke was not too pleased by his victory over Charles and it might be a good idea for Orlando to go away for a while.

Orlando hardly heard him, he was so eager to make sure of the name of the young woman who had thrown a chain around his neck and stolen his heart in such a short time. "Rosalind," Le Beau said, "the old duke's daughter. The other one is Celia, daughter of the present duke. But as I say, the duke really wants you gone."

All Orlando could say in answer was, "Heavenly Rosalind!"

"Love at first sight?" Celia and Rosalind were in their chambers at the palace, talking over the afternoon. "But is it really possible?" asked Celia.

Rosalind's eyes were shining, her cheeks rosy. "Oh, yes," she whispered. "Yes."

Just then the duke stormed into their room. "Mistress Rosalind, I want you out of this palace at once."

"What?" said both girls, astounded.

The duke was in one of his terrible tempers. It seemed to him that Rosalind had become too popular with everyone—more popular than Celia. Besides, he did not trust her. In ten days she must be twenty miles away or too bad for her.

"Father!" said Celia, "if this must be, you must banish me too. I cannot live without her friendship."

"You are a fool," was the duke's answer. Then, repeating that Rosalind must be gone at once, he stormed out as noisily as he had entered.

It did not take long for Celia to convince Rosalind that she was going with her, wherever she went.

But where should that be? asked Rosalind.

"The Forest of Arden!" said Celia. "Where else? That is where your father, who is also my dear uncle, lives in exile with his attendants. They will welcome us."

The girls decided to disguise themselves as country people for their journey. And rather than be two girls traveling together, Rosalind, because she was taller, should dress as a young man. Now they began to laugh as they decided on new names for themselves. Rosalind would be Ganymede and Celia would be Aliena. As they hurried about, collecting jewelry and what cash they had, the whole project began to seem not a banishment but an adventure into freedom.

Out in the Forest of Arden, the old duke, Rosalind's father, sat in the shade of a budding tree and smiled at the men around him. They were in exile, yes, but this life was not so bad.

"Sweet are the uses of adversity," said the duke, "which like the toad, ugly and venomous, wears yet a precious jewel in his head. And this our life, exempt from public haunt, finds tongues in trees, books in the running brooks, sermons in stones…and good in everything…I would not change it."

All the men around him nodded and smiled. Only one spoke up to say that it might be well enough for them, but wherever one went there was some suffering. For instance, they killed the deer for their meat. But some deer were wounded and not caught. Just a while ago he had seen Jacques, another of the duke's men, lamenting at the side of a wounded deer.

"Ah," said the duke, "our melancholy Jacques. But there is usually some sense in his lamenting. Let us go find him and hear his latest."

At the palace, the duke had discovered that the girls were gone, taking Touchstone the clown with them. Had they also taken Orlando, he wondered. In another of his rages he ordered his men to find out where the runaways had gone.

Actually, Orlando was making his own way to the Forest of Arden, along with his old servant, Adam. Filled with thoughts of Rosalind, he had no idea that she and Celia might be going to the same retreat.

By this time, the girls and Touchstone were at the edge of the forest and too tired and hungry to go any further. They were resting for a moment as two shepherds came by. The young one, Silvius, was talking about his love for someone named Phebe in a way that made Rosalind sympathize. His feelings were so like hers for Orlando. She sighed. But Celia and Touchstone were more interested in finding something to eat and some shelter.

The lovelorn young shepherd wandered off and Rosalind picked up courage to ask the older one if there was anyplace nearby where they might stay. By almost magical good luck, the shepherd knew of a little cottage that was for sale, along with its pasture and flocks. "Oh," cried Rosalind, "buy it for us and you shall be shepherd and everything will be splendid." She reached into the purse which hung at her doublet (she was dressed as a young man, don't forget) and gave the shepherd some gold pieces.

In a twinkling it was all accomplished. Ganymede and Aliena, and Touchstone too, had their own little cottage at the edge of the forest.

Things were not going so well for Orlando. As he and Adam made their way into the forest, Adam was near to fainting from weakness and hunger. Orlando laid him down by a tree and then ran out into the forest to see if he could find something for his old friend to eat. And so, by chance, he came upon the old duke and his man, feasting in a little glen.

"Hold!" cried Orlando. "Eat no more till necessity be served."

The duke looked up, astonished. "What sort of manners are these? Are you that hungry? If so, sit down in all civility and share our food."

Orlando was taken aback by such a gentle answer. He begged the duke's pardon and told him about his old and ailing servant. The duke said, "Go at once and bring him here." And with a grateful look Orlando went to do so.

"You see," the duke said, "we are not all alone unhappy... There are more woeful lots than ours."

At this, the melancholy Jacques began one of his philosophic speeches.

"All the world's a stage, and all the men and women merely players. They have their exits and their entrances and one man in his time plays many parts..." He went on, in his dreaming voice, to tell of childhood, young love, ambition—all the phases of a person's life. He had just arrived at old age when a person was "sans teeth, sans eyes, sans taste, sans everything," when Orlando returned, supporting Adam. Now everyone helped to make the old man comfortable and give him food. Someone started to sing…

"Blow, blow thou winter wind
Thou art not so unkind as man's ingratitude…"

But since everyone was well-fed and easy now, the sad words were not troubling. During the song, the duke and Orlando spoke quietly and Orlando told the duke his father's name.

"Sir Roland's son!" said the duke. "You are truly welcome here, you and your man, for as long as you wish to stay."

Had Orlando forgotten Rosalind during all of this? Not for a moment. Whatever he was doing, visions of her were in his mind and verses describing his feelings and her loveliness kept bubbling up. As soon as Adam was settled, he found some paper and wrote down one of the poems in his mind. Then, not knowing what else to do with it, he nailed it to a tree, after which he wrote another poem, and another, and these he nailed to trees also.

Of course, since Rosalind and Celia were living at the edge of the forest they soon found the poems. And since Rosalind's name was in every one, Celia was sure she knew who had written them. And then one morning she saw Orlando nailing a paper to a tree.

"You saw him? Orlando? Here in the forest?"

"Himself," said Celia.

"Alas!" cried Rosalind. "And me dressed as a youth. Will he know me—or not?"

Just then they both saw Orlando, not too far away. A teasing idea came into Rosalind's head. "I know. I shall speak to him as a saucy young man and—just see."

She ran toward Orlando, pulling her boy's cap further down to shadow her face.

After greeting him politely, she asked if he knew who was spoiling the trees of the forest by nailing up love-sick poems. He admitted he was the one who was love-sick and that he could think of no one, day or night, but Rosalind.

"I know how to cure this sort of love-sickness," Rosalind said. "And this is how. Every day you must visit me at the cottage I share with my sister, and you must pretend that I am Rosalind. Call me Rosalind. Make all the pretty speeches you would like to make to her. And then I will show you how proud, fantastical, shallow, and foolish a woman is. And so you will be cured."

"But I do not want to be cured."

"Well, at least try my plan. Come every day to woo me and call me Rosalind and see what happens."

It seemed rather foolish to Orlando but there was something appealing about the youth and he agreed to come each day for a class in curing love-sickness.

And now there began a real merry-go-round of love in the Forest of Arden, for Touchstone the clown had fallen in love with a shepherdess, Audrey. And Phebe, who was so beloved of the shepherd Silvius, had a few words with Rosalind, whom she thought was a young man named Ganymede, and fell madly in love with her.

Touchstone and Audrey wandered about together, talking of getting married. Phebe pined for Ganymede and sent her loving letters. And Rosalind waited only for Orlando's visit to the cottage.

She was very stern with him. "Men have died, and worms have eaten them, but not for love—not for love," she told him. And all the time she was more in love than ever.

Then came a day when Orlando did not appear as promised. Rosalind was too restless to stay in the cottage and she and Celia were walking in the woods when a strange young man approached them.

He said he was looking for a little cottage and a brother and sister named Ganymede and Aliena. Rosalind and Celia told him they were the ones he sought. He then brought out a bloody handkerchief from his pocket and handed it to Rosalind.

"He asked me to give this to you to show why he had failed in his appointment."

Rosalind stared at the bloody cloth and cried, "O, but what does this mean?"

The young man then told a tale of a man sleeping in the forest, and menaced by a lioness. Orlando, on his way to his appointment with Ganymede, saw the man and his danger. Coming closer, he saw the man was his brother.

"His brother!" said Celia.

"I have heard him speak of a brother, but not too kindly," said Rosalind.

"Nor should he have. But all the same, Orlando saw the danger to his brother, rushed at the lioness with his dagger, and finished her off. At which point, I awoke."

"*You* are his brother?" asked Celia.

"Was it you that wanted the wrestler to break his neck?" asked Rosalind.

"It was I, but it is not I," said the young man, who was indeed Oliver. "Something changed in me—changed forever—when I realized that the brother I had treated so badly would risk his life for me…When I told him that I too had been banished by the duke, Orlando took me to his cave to share it with him. Then, all of a sudden, murmuring "Rosalind," he fainted. Only then did I see that the lioness had clawed his arm. I restored him, bound his arm, and then he sent me with this kerchief to find the youth whom he calls Rosalind to explain…"

At this Rosalind fell to the ground in a faint. Together, Celia and Oliver roused her and took her to the cottage. When she was quite all right, Oliver still stayed on, his eyes fixed on Celia and hers on him. Celia, who had not believed in love at first sight, now did.

Celia could have her Oliver, who now wanted to make over all his father's estate to Orlando and live in the cottage with Celia as a shepherd. But what of Rosalind, still masquerading as a boy—and her love for Orlando?

Rosalind had an idea. If everyone, all the lovers, happy or unhappy, met at the duke's glen the next afternoon, she would work some magic to please everyone.

The next afternoon everyone was there, not quite sure what to think. Rosalind, her cap pulled well down over her eyes, stood before the duke, who was her father. She bowed to him and asked if she brought in Rosalind, his daughter, would he marry her to Orlando. "That I would," said the duke, "and I only wish I had a kingdom to give with her."

Rosalind turned to Orlando. "And would you have her?"

"That I would, were I of all kingdoms king."

Rosalind turned to the shepherdess, Phebe, who had fallen in love with her in her boyish garb. "You wish to marry me, if I be willing. But if you refuse to marry me, will you marry this loving shepherd here, Silvius?"

"If I refuse to marry you?" asked Phebe. "All right. Yes."

"Very well," said Rosalind. "I am leaving now for a minute or so but I will return soon." Then she beckoned to Celia and both girls ran off behind a screen of trees and bushes.

The duke looked very thoughtful. It seemed to him that the young man had a very familiar face. Orlando agreed that when he had first met him he had thought the lad must be Rosalind's brother. The duke and Orlando stared at each other, wondering.

Now Touchstone and Audrey joined the group and Touchstone and the melancholy Jacques had another of their wrangles.

Then, from behind the trees, came two pretty girls, dressed in filmy silk and ribbons. As they walked toward the others, one of the duke's men began to play on his viol. Another began to sing a cheerful song.

Only a moment of staring, and there was an outcry of joy from the duke and those around him. The duke had recognized his daughter, Rosalind, and held out his arms. So did Orlando.

And now there were four loving couples—Rosalind and Orlando, Celia and Oliver, Touchstone and Aubrey—and, wait —four? But Phebe only had to take one look at the transformed Ganymede and she threw herself into the arms of her loving swain, Silvius. So there were four loving couples, joining hands before the duke who now properly married them.

After that there was so much kissing and dancing and singing, one might have thought there was nothing more to wish for in this world.

But there was. A young man came into the glen from the forest. After he had introduced himself, he told his news. Duke Ferdinand, who had forced his older brother from the dukedom, had been on his way to the forest to find his brother and kill him when he met an old monk. Something in the monk's words had so impressed the younger duke that he put down his sword and joined the monastery as a convert. All the lands and goods he had taken from his older brother were now restored to him.

Everybody was fairly stunned by these tidings except Jacques, who said he thought he would join Duke Ferdinand in his monastery.

The old duke looked at Jacques and thought, "Well, maybe so." Then he clapped his hands and cried, "Proceed, proceed— surely these rites will end in true delights."

And isn't that the way a story should end—everyone happy? Just As You Like It.

othello

HEY CALLED HIM the Moor, for he was a big, dark man from Africa. And he was a hero to the citizens of Venice. Over and over again he had led their soldiers to defeat the Turks when they came darting in, trying to capture their rich city, laced with canals, or one of their island possessions.

But aside from the fact that he was a wonderful soldier, no one knew much else about Othello the Moor.

Except for Desdemona, the lovely daughter of Brabantio, one of the senators of Venice. The first time Othello had come to call on her father he had some moments with Desdemona alone and she had encouraged him to talk about himself and she had asked him to come again. He did come again—and again. Soon he and Desdemona had fallen in love. One afternoon they stole away to a magistrate and were married.

Othello knew there would be trouble with Brabantio when the marriage was discovered, but he felt no guilt. Desdemona had agreed they must present her father with an accomplished fact.

Worrying a little about Brabantio's reactions, Othello had no idea that he had anything to fear from his trusted lieutenant, Iago, whom he had just appointed his ensign, a sort of chief courier. He had no idea that Iago had wanted the post of first lieutenant, which Othello had just given to Cassio. Nor that Iago's mind was now roiling and moiling with schemes of how to get even with Othello.

Iago talked with his friend, Roderigo. "This romance of his with Desdemona... I saw the two of them in a gondola this evening, their arms around each other. Why not stir up old Brabantio against the Moor?"

Roderigo, who was in love with Desdemona himself, thought it was not a bad idea.

As it happened, they were quite near to Brabantio's house at the moment. They began shouting outside his door that his daughter had been stolen, and it did not take them long to stir up a real commotion. Brabantio and his servants came running out with torches.

"Your daughter—and the Moor!" Iago cried. "Perhaps they are married—who knows?"

"The Moor?" said Brabantio, and he began shouting at his servants to make ready to go with him and track down the villain.

At the height of the uproar, Iago stole away to look for Othello himself. He found him in front of the house where he lived, and now Iago was all concern and devotion, everything an ensign should be. "I wanted to kill old Brabantio myself for what he said about you, but I held myself back," said Iago.

"Just as well," said Othello.

"But now he and his men are coming after you. We must think what you should do."

Just then they saw a flare of torches and heard voices. "Brabantio!" said Iago. "You must go inside."

"Not I," said Othello. "I will meet him here."

But it was not Brabantio after all. Instead, it was Cassio, Othello's chief lieutenant, with some soldiers, bringing word that the duke wanted Othello at the palace at once. There was bad news from Cyprus. The Turks were starting another attack on that island.

Now came another flare of torches and babble of voices and this time it was Brabantio and his men, along with Roderigo.

Brabantio saw Othello and raised his sword and began shouting that the Moor had magicked his daughter. He called to his men to seize the Moor so he could take him to the duke and accuse him publicly.

"It will not be necessary," said Othello quietly. "I am already on my way to see the duke about the new trouble in Cyprus."

This silenced Brabantio for the moment and there seemed nothing to do but go along with Othello, Iago, Cassio, and Othello's men to the duke's palace.

Once in the duke's council room, however, Brabantio was in full cry. "He has magicked my daughter, bewitched her, given her strange potions, and stolen her from me," he shouted, pointing to Othello.

Othello admitted that he and Desdemona were married, but denied any witchcraft or enchantment. They loved each other. That was all.

The duke, really more anxious to get on with the business of the Turks, sighed. Perhaps they should send for the lady herself, he said. Iago, always ready to help, hurried off to get Desdemona.

While he was gone, Othello tried to explain to the duke how their love had come about. He told of their meetings and of how eager Desdemona was to hear of his adventures. "She pitied me for the dangers I had passed," he said, "and I loved her that she did pity me."

Then Iago was back with Desdemona, and Brabantio was shouting again that she had been enchanted or bewitched.

The duke turned to Desdemona for her answer.

Fair, rosy, and resolute, Desdemona went straight to Othello's side and took his hand. She loved her father but as everyone knew there came a time when children had to leave parents for a choice of their own. She had made her choice. "He is my lord," she said, smiling up at Othello.

"Well, so that's settled," said the duke, with some relief. "It is a grief to you, Brabantio, but what's done cannot be undone. Try to be grateful for a brave son-in-law. Now, Othello, to the business of the Turks."

The duke wanted Othello to sail for Cyprus that night. He would send further orders and dispatches by Cassio in the morning.

Othello nodded. He had only one request. He wanted proper accommodations for Desdemona while he was away, since it seemed unlikely that she would be happy in her father's house now. Then Desdemona spoke. What she wanted most was to go where Othello went. Would it not be possible for her to sail to Cyprus too, on one of the ships?

The duke wanted everything settled quickly. Yes, yes, of course. Iago could take her in his ship the next morning. And so it was arranged.

Iago and Roderigo were the last to leave the council room and Roderigo was in a dark mood. Now Desdemona was lost to him forever. He might as well drown himself.

Nonsense, said Iago. He was somewhat disappointed himself that the duke had accepted Othello's marriage so calmly and still trusted him so completely, so he was already scheming for some other way to injure Othello. How about making him jealous? Maybe of Cassio, his first lieutenant? Why not?

"The Moor is of a free and open nature, that thinks men honest that but seem to be so," said Iago, sure that one way or another he could lead Othello by the nose into some sort of misery.

The seas were stormy between Venice and Cyprus. While Othello was still out on the open waters fighting against the Turks, Cassio's ship finally limped into port. Later, Iago's ship came in, with Desdemona aboard along with Emilia, Iago's wife, whom he had brought to keep Desdemona company and be a maid to her. Iago was pleased to see Cassio kiss

Desdemona's hand when she came off the ship. A good beginning for his plotting.

And then before long, Othello's ship came in. There was
great rejoicing among all those gathered at the pier to hear that
once again he had beaten back the Turkish fleet. For Othello,
the chief joy was in seeing Desdemona again. "If after every
tempest come such calms, may the winds blow till they have
waken'd death…"

Iago watched as they went off to the governor's palace together. They were happy now, but he had his plans for the future. While the bells of the island rang, proclaiming the victory,
and a herald announced that next day would be a holiday to
celebrate the defeat of the Turks and the Moor's wedding, Iago
was whispering to Roderigo. "Did you notice Desdemona with
Cassio?" he said. And he implied that she was secretly enamored of the first lieutenant. When Roderigo looked unbeliev-
ing, Iago said, just watch—watch.

That night at the victory party, Iago first set out to make
Roderigo tipsy. Then he went to work on Cassio, whom Othello
had appointed to watch on the walls that night. Iago was
pleased to see he was quite addled when he went out to keep the
watch. Soon he sent Roderigo out after him and in no time
there were sounds of a fight. Then Roderigo was running into
the hall with Cassio pursuing him, beating at him with his
sword.

Alarmed, an aide named Montano tried to stop the fight and
was wounded by Cassio's sword. In the tumult someone rang an
alarm bell. Iago told Roderigo to run away and turned back to
Cassio and Montano.

By that time Othello and some of his men were hurrying in.
What was wrong?

Othello was shocked by the signs of drinking and brawling. Who had begun this disgraceful business? he asked. So Iago began a long, made-up story about Cassio pursuing some unknown person who had been crying for help.

The more Iago talked, the sadder and surer Othello became. Iago was making up this story to spare Cassio and this was very generous of him. "Your honesty and love try to mince matters," he said, but he was not fooled. He turned to Cassio. "Cassio, I love thee. But nevermore be officer of mine."

It was all turning out just as Iago had hoped. Desdemona came in to see what had happened. Othello reassured her and they left together. Now Iago could turn all his attention to Cassio, who was crushed. Stripped of his rank, his reputation was gone. It was the immortal part of himself—gone, gone. He cursed the wine that had stolen away his wits. Why did men put such an enemy in their mouths?

Come, come, said Iago. Every man gets drunk now and then. The thing to do now was to win Othello's pardon and the best way to accomplish that was to get Desdemona to plead for him. The Moor so doted on her that he would surely grant any favor she asked. Cassio looked gratefully at Iago. Thank you, he said, and then, as he limped away, "Good night, honest Iago."

By now, Iago was feeling very pleased with himself. "Who says I play the villain when this advice I give is so free and honest?" he muttered. Then he pondered his next steps. He saw Desdemona pleading for Cassio while he himself whispered innuendos into Othello's ear. But now he thought he needed the help of his wife, Emilia, in his schemes. He went to talk to her.

Next day, as Desdemona sat in the sunny arbor outside the palace, Emilia came to her begging that she would see Cassio privately. Well, of course, said Desdemona.

So Cassio came to Desdemona and asked for her help, which

she gladly promised to give. And of course it was not by accident that Iago managed to have Othello nearby as Cassio left the arbor. Iago shook his head in a worried way.

Othello had never given a thought to Cassio's friendship with Desdemona. But now as Iago spoke of how Cassio had left in such a guilty way Othello could not help frowning and wondering a little.

Desdemona, of course, had no idea that she was walking in on such a conversation when she came to Othello begging that he restore Cassio to his post. Othello was gentle with her, but she kept insisting. "Please? Soon?"

"I can deny thee nothing," he said finally, "but just now leave me a little time to myself."

With Desdemona gone, Iago persisted in his suspicious remarks until he really was beginning to worry Othello. At which point, Iago warned him against jealousy, "the green-eyed monster." The warning only increased Othello's alarm. He tried to hold it in check but asked Iago to keep watch on Cassio and Desdemona.

And then came the business of the handkerchief, made to order for Iago. Just a pretty embroidered handkerchief that Othello had given to Desdemona before their marriage. That evening Othello had a headache. Desdemona said she would bind it with her handkerchief, but it turned out to be too small. As they went into another room to find something larger, Desdemona dropped the handkerchief without knowing it.

Emilia picked it up and took it to Iago. He smiled and soon had dropped it in Cassio's room.

That night, as Othello roamed the palace, unable to sleep, Iago kept working on his fears and soon brought up the subject of the handkerchief, a pretty thing, embroidered with strawberries.

"I gave her such a one. It was my first gift to her," said Othello.

"So," said Iago, "I did not know it was your wife's, but today I saw Cassio wipe his beard with it."

Now Othello suddenly lost all his calm and was like a man possessed. He knelt to swear revenge on a wife who betrayed him, and Iago knelt beside him.

"Proof! Proof!" cried Othello. And now Iago made up a tale of spending a night once with Cassio and hearing Cassio speak Desdemona's name in his sleep.

Still Othello tried to restrain himself. The next day he asked Desdemona for the handkerchief. She said she did not have it with her. A pity, said Othello, for there had been magic woven into the web of that handkerchief. Really? said Desdemona. She would do her best to find it.

And then, in all innocence, she began once more to plead with Othello to restore Cassio to his post.

It was too much. Othello stormed away, leaving Desdemona to wonder how she had offended him.

By now, all that Iago had to do was talk a great deal about his own devotion to Othello and his sorrow that he should be so troubled.

Othello began to go a little crazy. A messenger came from Venice and was so disturbed by Othello's behavior that he thought he should report back to the duke that Othello was no longer fit for service. Twice during the next day, Othello fainted. He had always been a man so quiet and steady that this behavior astonished everyone.

Desdemona, distracted, asked Emilia what could have gone wrong. Why was Othello so cold and angry with her? Jealousy makes men do strange things, Emilia answered. "But why should he be jealous?" asked Desdemona desperately. "I never gave him any cause." Then, seeing Iago, she ran to him to ask for help in winning back her lord.

Of course, said Iago, soothing her, but actually he was busy with some new scheming. It was beginning to seem likely that Othello would be removed as governor of Cyprus and Cassio appointed in his place. Now Iago conferred with Roderigo and talked him into killing Cassio at the earliest opportunity.

One man plotting, plotting—and a whole palace was in a tumult.

"Go to bed," Othello shouted at Desdemona when she approached him wistfully. And Desdemona obediently went off to her room.

Emilia was alarmed by her mood of despair. "I would you had never met that man," she said.

"I do not wish that," said Desdemona. "Even now, his stubbornness, his cheeks, his frowns, are pleasing to me."

Emilia could only sniff at that and then go on spreading the bed with the wedding sheets as Desdemona had asked her to do.

Desdemona began to sing a plaintive song she remembered from her childhood, about a maiden disappointed in love, sitting by a riverbank and singing, "Willow, willow, willow . . ."

Emilia grew still more distressed. She began to talk about the wrongs women suffered. "Let husbands know their wives have sense like them, they see and smell and have their palates both for sweet and sour . . . The ills we do, their ills instruct us so. . ."

Desdemona was not interested in such talk. "Willow, willow, willow," she sang, and then she bade Emilia good night.

Outside, on a dark lane outside the palace, Iago was whispering to Roderigo, stiffening his courage to kill Cassio. They heard footsteps approaching. "Here he comes," said Iago. "Now—kill him, kill him!" he said as Cassio came abreast of them.

Roderigo lunged and missed. Cassio drew his sword and managed to stab Roderigo. Iago lunged at Cassio, stabbed him in the leg, and then fled. Cassio fell to the ground crying, "Murder! murder!"

His cries brought Othello and several others hurrying from the palace. Cassio moaned and said he thought one of his attackers was still nearby.

Just then, Iago, always helpful, came running with a torch. He stopped by Roderigo, moaning with the wound Cassio had given him. And quickly Iago stabbed Roderigo to death.

Leaving this bloody scene, Othello made his way slowly to the bedroom he shared with Desdemona. She was asleep, fair and lovely in the wedding sheets. He stared at her, his soul in torment.

"I'll not shed her blood, nor scar that whiter skin of hers than snow . . . yet she must die, else she'll betray more men . . ."

He put his hands over his eyes for a moment. "Put out the light, and then put out the light . . ." He dropped his hands and looked at her again and knelt to kiss her. She woke. "Have you said your prayers, Desdemona?" he asked.

Sleepy-eyed, she looked at him. "But yes, of course."

"And confessed your sins?"

"What sins?"

"Your love for Cassio, proved by that handkerchief you gave him."

"My lord, my lord, I never gave him the handkerchief. He must have found it. Send for him and ask him."

"No use. He is dead."

"O, no, how sad."

"Ah, so now you weep for him before my eyes."

"No, no."

But it was too late. All the poisons Iago had poured into

Othello's ears had deranged both his sense and spirit. Scarcely knowing what he did, he picked up a pillow and held it with all his strength over Desdemona's face.

What use now for Emilia to rush in and, horrified by what she saw, try to convince Othello of Desdemona's innocence? Iago was right behind her, ready to stab his own wife before she could tell Othello the truth. The room was filling up with people, crying out in shock and dismay. And one man, of a certain authority, saying Othello must be arrested.

Othello spoke quietly now. Yes, the whole matter must be reported in Venice but when it was, would they mention the services he had done the state in the past, and then speak also "of one who loved not wisely but too well."

And then before anyone could stop him, he was beside the bed, stabbing himself. Then as he sank to his knees, he leaned over to kiss Desdemona.

"I kiss'd thee ere I kill'd thee; no way but this: killing myself, to die upon a kiss."

antony and and cleopatra

ND NOW WE ARE in Egypt—ancient Egypt, in the days when Rome's great general, Marc Antony, had fallen under the spell of the enchanting queen, Cleopatra.

Antony's hair was grizzled, his face somewhat lined. Cleopatra was no longer a child-queen but a full woman. Still they were beautiful together, beautiful to each other, and they spent their days and nights in love and pleasure, in the great palace at Alexandria, on some lavishly appointed boat on the river Nile, or riding about through the city in a gilded chariot, smiling on the citizens.

From time to time, messengers came to Antony from Rome bearing letters that begged him to return. Not only was he general of the army, he was one of the three triumvirs who ruled the Roman world, east, west, north, and south. The other two, Octavius Caesar and Lepidus, were dismayed by Antony's behavior in Egypt. Besides, he was needed at home.

Antony sent the messengers away and ignored the letters. Sometimes Cleopatra scolded him for this. "You should read the letters, you know. Perhaps you should return. Perhaps your wife, Fulvia, wants you." Then suddenly she would be fiercely jealous and it would be all Antony could do to reassure her that she was his only love, his world. She spun him like a top, flinging him away from her but as surely drawing him back.

If he was absent from her for a while, she sent her maid, Charmian, to find him. "If he is sad, tell him I am merry. If he is merry, tell him I am sad." Her contradictions were part of her fascination.

But then came some messengers that Antony could not ignore. They brought the news that Antony's wife, Fulvia, had joined with his brother in an ill-fated rebellion and that now she was dead. Nor was that all. Pompey, a high-ranking Roman who thought he had been overlooked in the parcelling out of power, was rebelling against the triumvirs. He had put together a strong fleet and was sailing about, nipping off various islands and other territories under Roman rule and claiming them for his own. It appeared now that he was approaching Rome itself.

Antony seemed to wake from a dream. He called for his men to begin packing and then went to Cleopatra. It was not easy to tell her he was leaving.

"O, I am betrayed," she cried.

Antony tried to explain that he really was needed in Rome. She would not listen. "O, most false love. I am ill. I am ill."

"My precious queen, forbear," Antony begged. "Surely you know my love by now and that I will return." But Cleopatra would not be pacified and Antony had to leave with her lamentations in his ears.

Still, he was hardly out of sight before she was crying, "O, bring me mandragora, Charmian, a soothing syrup that I may sleep away the time my Antony is away." But of course she did not sleep. As the days passed she agitated herself by wondering where Antony was at that moment. On a horse somewhere? On a ship? A messenger arrived with a great pearl for her that Antony had sent as a parting gift. "O, how was he?" cried Cleopatra. "How did he look? Was he merry or sad?" Then she sat down to write another letter to him, as she did several times a day, posting them off by messengers who must try to catch up with Antony on his way to Rome.

Rome . . . It was a different world from Alexandria. Cold, white marble buildings glittered on the hilltops. Cold, pale men plotted the course of the empire and fought for power among themselves.

Octavius Caesar, son of the late, great Julius Caesar, was such a cool, pale man, but Antony's long stay in Egypt and his infatu-ation with Cleopatra had roused him to a certain anger. He talked to Lepidus about the man Antony had been—the great-est soldier in the world, able to turn defeat into victory over and over again, a man who was ready for any hardship and who could withstand any pain. But now he was throwing away all those qualities in voluptuous living.

A messenger came in to report that Pompey's fleet was grow-ing in strength and that two famous pirates were roaming the Italian coast, looting almost at will. Caesar, usually so con-trolled, hit his palms together. "Antony, leave your revels and get back to Rome!"

But Antony was on his way and soon he was there. Along with his loyal first lieutenant, Enobarbus, he stood before Cae-sar, not penitent, but sorry that there had been so many difficul-ties during his absence. He regretted the brief revolt of his brother and his late wife. He knew there was reason to be trou-bled by Pompey's rebellion. He spoke quietly but it was clear he had come back to do his part in subduing Pompey.

Caesar sighed, looked at Antony, and looked away. He did not doubt his words. But he wished there were some way to bind him—some hoop that would stretch from one edge of the world to the other.

Agrippa, one of Caesar's advisors, spoke up. Caesar had an unmarried sister, Octavia. Marc Antony was now a widower.

Caesar interrupted. "Cleopatra would not like to hear that."

Marc Antony still spoke quietly. "I am not married, Caesar. Let Agrippa speak further."

And so Agrippa suggested that Antony marry Octavia, a vir-tuous woman who would do him honor. With such a marriage, Caesar and Antony would become brothers, and in such a rela-tionship all jealousies and differences could be forgotten.

"What says Caesar?" asked Marc Antony.

"Not till I hear how Antony is touched," said Caesar. There was a pause. Then, "If it can be so, let it," said Antony.

What had happened to Antony? Had he forgotten all his vows to Cleopatra so swiftly? Or was it just that Antony was in Rome now, thinking like a Roman?

Caesar clasped Antony's hand. The marriage would be arranged. He was very pleased. Now they must talk privately of Pompey, who had sent messages from the port city of Misenum that he would like a meeting.

"Very well," said Antony, and he followed Caesar into an inner room.

Enobarbus was left with Agrippa. "What was it like in Egypt?" asked Agrippa curiously.

"Ah," said Enobarbas, "feasting night and day, feasting and music and dancing."

"And Cleopatra?" asked Agrippa.

Enobarbus closed his eyes, remembering the first time he had seen Cleopatra, coming up the river.

> "The barge she sat in, like a burnish'd throne,
> Burned on the water: the poop was beaten gold;
> Purple the sails and so perfumed
> That the winds were love-sick with them."

Agrippa was fascinated. He wanted to hear more and more and Enobarbus was happy to oblige.

Finally Agrippa sighed. "Now Antony must leave her utterly."

Enobarbus shook his head. "Never. He will not. Age cannot wither her, nor custom stale her infinite variety."

Agrippa stared and wondered.

Whatever Enobarbus predicted, preparations for Antony's

marriage went on. Antony was taken to meet Octavia, a quiet lady, cool and pale as her brother. He spoke graciously to her, admitting that his life as a soldier and triumvir would take him away from her for long periods, but whatever she had heard of his past life, with her all would be done by the rule.

It was strange that right after leaving Octavia, Antony should meet an old soothsayer who had followed him from Egypt.

"Hie you to Egypt," mumbled the soothsayer.

"So?" said Antony. Then he asked, "Whose fortunes shall rise higher, mine or Caesar's?"

"Caesar's," said the soothsayer. "Your angel becomes a spirit of fear when near him. When you play at any game with him he beats you against the odds. Therefore keep a space between you."

"Ah, get along with you," said Antony. But after the soothsayer had shuffled off, he could not help thinking of how many times Caesar did beat him when they played any games together. Even the dice seemed to favor him always. Well, so be it. He would go back to Egypt—some day. But he had made commitments here. He went to find one of his lieutenants whom he was sending with a regiment to deal with the Parthians. Beyond that, he had other promises to keep.

A messenger brought Cleopatra word of Antony's marriage. She sat on her gilded throne and stared at the man in disbelief. He repeated, "Madam, he's married to Octavia."

She swung out a hand and struck him down.

He scrambled to his feet. "Good madam, patience," he said. "I that do bring the news made not the match."

But now Cleopatra sprang up and grabbed his shoulders and shook him like a rag. "Say it is not so!"

"He's—married—madam," the messenger said breathlessly.

"Rogue," cried Cleopatra and she reached for the jeweled dagger she wore at her belt.

At this her maid Charmian came running and the messenger pulled himself away and dashed from the room.

"Good madam," said Charmian, "the man is innocent."

"Ahh, innocent!" sneered Cleopatra. But then she wanted the messenger back again and now she promised not to hurt him.

So the messenger came back to repeat his refrain. Antony was married to Octavia. At last Cleopatra was ready to dismiss the poor man. But as soon as he was gone she sent a servant running after him. She wanted to know everything about Octavia. How old she was, how tall, the color of her hair. Let him find out all that and return.

Then Cleopatra collapsed in tears on Charmian's shoulder. "Pity me, Charmian. But do not speak to me. Take me to my chamber."

And Antony? He was first in one place, then another. He was at Misenum with Caesar and Lepidus to meet with Pompey and talk about the possibility of a truce. Pompey chose to celebrate the meeting with a splendid banquet aboard his galley. There was so much food and drink—especially drink—that Lepidus had to be carried out before the banquet was over. But little was accomplished in the way of a truce.

Then Antony was in Rome with Caesar, where he was dismayed to hear Caesar speaking to the Senate and the populace as though he, Antony, hardly existed. Everything turned on what Caesar was doing—the new war he was making on Pompey, a new will he was writing (with no mention of Antony). It was very strange.

Then Antony was off to Athens where he had been posted. Octavia was already there and she was distressed to hear about the happenings in Rome. Was she to be torn between loyalty to her husband and her brother? She begged Antony that she might go to Rome and try to make things better between the two of them. Antony did not think it would do much good but he made no objection.

And then, soon after Octavia had left for Rome, Antony was on his way to Egypt—and Cleopatra.

They greeted each other with tears of joy. All Cleopatra's rages were forgotten. There were no questions about what Antony had hoped to accomplish in Rome. They were simply caught up in the happiness of being together again.

In Rome, Caesar frowned as he heard reports from his own men in Alexandria. Antony and Cleopatra were enthroned publicly on chairs of gold. Antony, as triumvir of the east, had declared Cleopatra absolute queen of Egypt and a host of smaller countries around it. How dare he, thought Caesar. Then he considered the situation. Pompey was no longer a threat. In fact, Pompey had been murdered by one of his own officers. After that it had been easy to disperse his followers. As for Lepidus, who had been ill ever since the banquet on Pompey's galley, Caesar had simply removed him from office. Now only Antony stood between Caesar and absolute power. But he would not do so for long, thought Caesar, rubbing his pale hands together. Antony might be invincible on land but he might easily be defeated at sea. Yes, that would be the way to go after him—by sea.

We meet Caesar at *sea*? Enobarbus was shocked when he heard Antony's decision. All Antony's officers and men were shocked. But there they were at Actium, where Antony's fleet was anchored along with Cleopatra's, ready to sail out to challenge Caesar's.

What was more, Cleopatra was with them, and Enobarbus thought this a terrible mistake also. She would distract Antony when he needed all his wits for battle. Cleopatra heard him muttering and was not pleased. "As head of my kingdom, I will appear as a man would do. Speak not against it. I will not stay behind."

Then Antony was with them, bringing news that Caesar's ships were approaching with much greater speed than expected. He would soon be near their coast. "And so we will fight him by sea," said Antony.

"By sea, what else," said Cleopatra.

In vain, Antony's officers tried to dissuade him. "Our strength is ever on land, sir, not on the sea." Antony waved them away. He told his generals to hold the forces in camp. "We'll to sea. To sea!"

And so there came about the great disaster. Enobarbus and some fellow officers watched from the shore. As an arm of Caesar's fleet swung about in a flanking movement, the Egyptian ship bearing Cleopatra turned and tacked in to shore. Then, as Enobarbus watched in horror, the lead Roman vessel, with Antony aboard, also turned to follow Cleopatra's ship to safety. With the two lead ships gone, the rest of Anthony's and Cleopatra's fleets were soon routed.

"O, whither hast thou led me, Egypt?" Antony cried in despair. He and Cleopatra were back in Alexandria, along with most of their land forces.

"O, my lord, my lord, forgive my fearful sails! I little thought you would have followed."

"Egypt, thou knowest too well my heart was to thy rudder tied. . ."

"Pardon, pardon," whispered Cleopatra.

"Ah, well," said Antony. "It is done. Give me a kiss."

So for a while they were happy again with each other, but neither could escape the rising tension. Caesar had followed them to the Egyptian coast. What would his next move be?

As it turned out, Caesar's next move was to send an envoy to Cleopatra, promising her that if she would forswear Antony and put herself under his protection, she could still keep her kingdom and crown.

For some reason best known to her contrary self, Cleopatra chose to answer the envoy sweetly, half promising her surrender. The envoy was kissing her hand when Antony appeared.

At the sight of Cleopatra smiling down at Caesar's man, Antony fell into a rage of his own. He shouted at Cleopatra's attendants, "Take this man away and whip him."

The attendants went off with the Roman envoy and now Antony was shouting at Cleopatra. So this was all her talk of love meant! Behind his back she was bargaining with Caesar. He raved on and on. But Cleopatra listened so humbly and then suddenly was telling him of her love in such a lavish way that they were soon in each other's arms again. Antony told her that tomorrow he would fight Caesar on land and be the Antony of old, who could not be defeated. Meantime, it was Cleopatra's birthday. Let there be a banquet tonight with music and feasting as in the happier days. "Yes," said Cleopatra, "since my lord is Antony again, I will be Cleopatra."

There was revelry that night in the palace. But it was revelry in which Enobarbus did not join. He had been watching Antony's distracted behavior with more and more concern. Antony raged like a dying lion. Perhaps ... perhaps, for his own survival, it would be as well if he, Enobarbus, went over to Caesar's camp. He slipped quietly into the night.

The feasting had hardly ended when the dawn came. Antony called for his armor. "No sleep at all, my lord?" asked Cleopatra.

"No," he said.

"Then let me help you put on your armor," she said. Soon he was ready.

Drums were beating, trumpets blowing, in both Antony's camp and Caesar's. Antony's appearance cheered his men and Antony himself was full of confidence until an aide told him of Enobarbus's defection. "Enobarbus?" said Antony, "O, no." It seemed a bad omen, but he pushed that thought aside, rallied his men, and led the charge forward toward the first line of Caesar's men.

The fighting went on all day, swords flashing, daggers chopping, men falling, rising again, falling, and sometimes not rising again. By dusk, Antony was content that he had driven all of Caesar's men back to their camp by the sea. At the palace, Antony was jubilant and Cleopatra met his mood, talking of tomorrow's final victory and how they would celebrate.

That night Enobarbus, sick at heart for having deserted Antony, fell on his sword and killed himself.

Antony knew nothing of that when he joined his troops at dawn, but somehow the mood was darker than it had been yesterday. An aide told him of a strange omen. Swallows were building their nests in the sails of Cleopatra's ships. The soothsayers were not sure what that meant but it looked bad. And today Caesar had chosen to fight at sea as well as on land.

In a few hours the worst was known. Caesar's fleet had wellnigh destroyed Antony's ships and Cleopatra's.

Antony staggered inland from the beachhead where he had been watching. "All is lost. All." Suddenly he began to blame Cleopatra. She had betrayed him and was in league with Caesar.

At this moment Cleopatra ran to him. Antony shouted at her like a madman. "Avaunt! Be gone!"

"My lord," she whispered, "why are you angry?"

He flung wild accusations at her. Let Caesar take her to Rome, he said, and display her in triumph at his side.

Cleopatra turned and fled.

Back with Charmian and her women Cleopatra cried, "What shall I do? O, he is mad."

Between them, they decided that she should go to the monument, a curious building outside the palace, which had no doors or windows on the ground floor so that all entrance had to be made by ladder or sling-seat. "Yes, yes," cried Cleopatra, "to the monument. Then go tell Antony I have slain myself. And the last word I spoke was Antony."

The news was brought to Antony. "Dead?" he whispered. "Dead?"

All his tortured blame of her was forgotten. He spoke as one stunned. "I shall o'er take thee, Cleopatra." He called an aide, Eros, who was almost as close as Enobarbus had been. He asked Eros to kill him. Eros protested—once, twice, and again. When Antony insisted, Eros said, "Then turn your head." Antony did so and Eros fell on his sword himself. Antony turned and saw.

"O, no, no," he said. "Thrice-nobler than myself. You teach me what I should do."

Now Antony drew his own sword, held it before him, and fell upon it. But, alas, he did not find death at a single stroke. He lay bleeding and calling feebly for the guards to come and finish him off.

The guards came and stared in horror. And then there came also a messenger from Cleopatra who was regretting the previous message she had sent and fearing what it might lead Antony to do. She wanted to see him at the monument.

"Not dead," murmured Antony. "Then bear me, good

friends, where Cleopatra bides. It is the last service that I shall command of you."

The guards lifted Antony and carried him to the monument. Cleopatra and Charmian let down a sort of hammock and the guards placed Antony in it. Cleopatra and Charmian strained to lift his heavy weight. "Help me, my women," Cleopatra gasped. "Help, good friends."

At last he was safely inside the second-floor room. He lay on the floor looking up at Cleopatra. "I am dying, Egypt, dying," he said, "but I put off death a while for one more kiss." She bent over him and they spoke gently and kissed, and then he died.

"O, now there is nothing left remarkable beneath the visiting moon," said Cleopatra, and she sank over Antony's body.

Cleopatra had played at killing herself many times to get attention or win her own way. This time, she thought, there will be no pretending. But how should it be done, with all the dignity of a queen?

She allowed herself to be raised from Antony's body and taken to another room.

She stood when Caesar came up a ladder to her quarters and then she knelt before him to offer her allegiance. Caesar begged her to rise. He promised her she would lose nothing of her royalty when she came with him to Rome. He was gentle and sympathetic. But as Cleopatra watched him go she was sure he spoke nothing but words. Meantime, she had whispered an errand to Charmian, who had gone to do her bidding.

After Caesar had left, she waited quietly, telling Iras, another of her maids, how dreadful it would be to be exhibited in triumph in Rome. At last the person came that she was waiting for—a countryman bearing a basket of figs.

"Have you the pretty worm of Nilus there, that kills and pains not?"

ANTONY AND CLEOPATRA

"Truly," said the countryman. "But he is indeed dangerous."
He told of how the bite of an asp had killed a certain woman
instantly.

"Yes, enough. Farewell," said Cleopatra. She called for Charmian and Iras to bring her crown and robes. Arrayed in them,
she sat in a great seat with the basket of figs in her lap. She rum-
maged in it for one of the small poisonous snakes called asps.
She found one and put it to her breast.

"Methinks I hear Antony call. I see him rouse himself to
praise my noble act . . ." She called Charmian and Iras to her to
kiss them farewell. Then she found another asp in the basket of
figs and put it on her arm. "As sweet as balm, as soft as air, as
gentle, O, Antony—" And so she died as she had wished, quietly, with the dignity that befitted a queen.

A guard came hurrying in to say that Caesar was visiting
again. "He comes too late," said Charmian, finding an asp and
applying it to her arm. Iras did the same. By the time Caesar
entered, all was still. The queen and her two women were dead.

Caesar stopped and stared. Then he spoke softly. "Bravest at
the last, she levelled at our purposes, and being royal, took her
own way."

After that, he fussed about trying to discover the poison she
had used. There seemed no clue until one of his men discovered
the slimy trail left by the asps.

"So," said Caesar. And then, in his victory over both Antony
and Cleopatra, he did speak some understanding and sympathetic words.

"Take her and her women from the monument. She shall be
buried by her Antony. No grave upon the earth shall clip in it a
pair so famous."

a mid-summer night's dream

LORD, WHAT FOOLS these mortals be," said Puck. He was a mischievous elf who lived in the forest just beyond Athens, and indeed, on this particular midsummer night, the mortals who were roaming about in the forest were behaving rather foolishly.

Of course, Puck himself had helped things along.

There were, for instance, four young people from Athens wandering the woods in a romantic muddle.

It had started when Hermia and Lysander, very much in love, decided to elope to another city where they could marry in spite of Hermia's father's insistence that she marry Demetrius.

Demetrius, newly smitten by Hermia, had followed along at a distance. And after him came Helena, whom he once had loved, and who was desperate to win him back.

A muddle already? Wait.

Oberon, king of the fairies, had seen the unhappy Helena following Demetrius, seen her rebuffed by him whenever she approached, and Oberon felt sorry for her. He had with him a magic potion, brewed from a flower called love-in-idleness. Once it was smeared on the eyelids of a sleeper, the sleeper would fall madly in love with whatever person he saw first on awakening. Oberon summoned Puck and told him to find the young Athenian and if he lay down to sleep, to smear his eyelids with the potion so that when he woke and saw Helena nearby he would love her beyond any other.

So far, so good. Except that Puck did not know that there were two young men from Athens in the forest that night and he found the wrong one—Lysander—sleeping under a tree, with Hermia out of sight on the other side of the trunk. Puck smeared the potion on Lysander's eyelids.

And then, as luck would have it, Helena was nearby when Lysander awoke. He jumped to his feet, all his love for Hermia forgotten, and began to pour out adoring words.

This was not at all what Helena wanted and she tried to escape him. It certainly was not what Hermia wanted. She woke from her nap to find her lover chasing Helena, who was running to find Demetrius if she could.

A real muddle now.

But there were some other mortals in the forest that night, capable of their own foolishness. Six workmen had come to a little glen to rehearse a play which they were going to perform for the duke's wedding festivities. They knew precious little about putting on a play but were trying to do their best. The play called for two lovers, Pyramus and Thisbe, to speak through a chink in a wall. They wondered how they could arrange such an effect in the duke's great hall, and then inspiration struck. One of them would smear himself with plaster, announce himself a wall, and hold his fingers apart to represent the chink. The play was supposed take place by moonlight. Again—inspiration! Another of the workmen would hold a lantern and proclaim himself moonshine.

Now, in the glen, they began a real rehearsal. Bottom, the weaver, who was playing Pyramus, the hero, rattled off his first speech in good order. Then he retired behind a hawthorn hedge as Quince, the self-appointed director, had told him to do to wait for his cue.

How could Bottom know that Titania, queen of the fairies, was sleeping in a cradle of leaves behind those hedges?

But Puck knew, of course. In fact, Puck had been sent there by Oberon, who was cross with his queen at the moment. Puck had been instructed to smear Titania's eyelids with the magic potion that would make her fall in love with the first creature she saw on awakening. Puck had already applied the potion when Bottom came around to listen for his cue. Now Puck had a notion for some mischief of his own. In a twinkling he had covered Bottom's head with a donkey's.

Quince called for Bottom to come back for his next speech. All unaware of any transformation in his appearance, Bottom came hurrying out.

"O, no! O, horror! O, what can this be?" the workmen cried as they saw him. In amazement and terror they all took to their heels.

Bottom was left alone and bewildered. Why had they stared so and then run away? "They're just trying to make a donkey of me. Well, I'll show them I'm not afraid."

He began to sing a cheerful song and his voice wakened the sleeping Titania. Opening her eyes, she listened to the singing and thought it beautiful. She rose from her bed of leaves and hurried around the hedge to find the singer—Bottom.

She clapped her hands. "O, lovely, lovely."

Bottom broke off his song mid-note and stared. Never in his life had he seen anything like this glorious fairy queen, her hair glittering with dewdrop diamonds, her gown all filmy and fluttery as mist in the moonlight.

"O, sing again, gentle mortal," cried Titania. She stared at him with delight. "O, I love you. I love you."

Bottom was astounded, to say the least. But he was a stout-hearted fellow, after all, ready to make the best of things. If this fabulous creature approved of him, why argue?

Soon Titania was seated on the grass with Bottom's donkey head in her lap. She was stroking and caressing his hairy forehead and long ears. She was calling her handmaidens to bring him fruit, sweetmeats, and anything his heart desired. "O, I dote on you," she whispered. "How beautiful you are."

Well, if it were all like a dream to Bottom for the next few hours he reveled in his good fortune.

But by this time Oberon had discovered the mistake Puck had made with the young Athenian lover and the confusion that had resulted. Lysander pursuing Helena, Hermia distracted, Helena distracted.

"You will have to go and undo that magic," said the fairy king to Puck, "and see that the proper lovers are united."

Meantime, he looked at Titania asleep with Bottom's donkey head in her lap and decided that his punishment of her had gone far enough. "First, though," said Oberon, "we will undo this enchantment."

He leaned over Titania. "Be as thou was wont to be, see as thou was wont to see. Now, my Titania, wake you, my sweet love."

The fairy queen opened her eyes. "My Oberon," she said. "What visions I have seen. I thought I was enamored of an ass."

"There lies your love," said Oberon, pointing to Bottom who had rolled over onto the grass, still sleeping.

"How came such a thing to pass?" asked Titania.

"Never mind. We are friends again now and tomorrow night we may even visit the duke's palace to add our blessing to his wedding festivities."

Then as he and Titania walked away, he told Puck to remove Bottom's donkey head, wake him up, and send him home with no memory of what had happened, except perhaps as a dream. He also reminded him not to forget to straighten out the muddle of the young lovers.

And so it came about that everything worked out beautifully. Puck restored Bottom's natural appearance and saw him on his way home. Then he found the four confused lovers sleeping off their fatigue and this time he distributed his magic potion more carefully. Lysander awoke and saw his dear Hermia by his side and knew he had never loved anyone but her. Demetrius awoke